E. E. CUMMINGS

E. E. CUMMINGS

by Catherine Reef

Clarion Books   New York

Clarion Books
a Houghton Mifflin Company imprint
215 Park Avenue South, New York, NY 10003
Copyright © 2006 by Catherine Reef

The text was set in 13-point Granjon.

For information about permission to reproduce selections from this book,
write to Permissions, Houghton Mifflin Company,
215 Park Avenue South, New York, NY 10003.

www.clarionbooks.com

Printed in the U.S.A.

Library of Congress Cataloging-in-Publication Data

Reef, Catherine.
E. E. Cummings / by Catherine Reef.
p. cm.
Includes bibliographical references and index.
ISBN-13: 978-0-618-56849-9
ISBN-10: 0-618-56849-2
1. Cummings, E. E. (Edward Estlin), 1894–1962. 2. Poets, American—
20th century—Biography—Juvenile literature. I. Title.
PS3505.U334Z83 2006
811′.52—dc22
2006010453

MP 10 9 8 7 6 5 4 3 2 1

For old friends

(Who:
Loves;
Creates,
Imagines)
OPENS

E. E. Cummings

contents

little i

who are you,little i

(five or six years old)
peering from some high

window;at the gold

of november sunset . . .

E.E. Cummings wrote these lines at the end of his life, on a day when he looked far into his memory and spied himself as a child in Cambridge, Massachusetts.

From the third story of the Cummings home, three dormer windows looked out over apple and cherry trees, their branches bare in November. A child might gaze down on the grassy square at the spot where Irving, Scott, and Farrar streets met. In spring, melting snow filled this square with a glorious puddle that turned the neighborhood children into splashing ducks.

In spring, a child might also spot the balloon man, who whistled as he walked the streets. His bright balloons tugged against their strings as they reached for the sky, resembling the tulips that brightened Cambridge gardens with their colorful blossoms atop straight stems.

A childhood portrait of Estlin Cummings by the Boston artist Charles Sydney Hopkinson.

The Cummings home at 104 Irving Street, Cambridge.

E. E. Cummings was born in this house, at 104 Irving Street on October 14, 1894. He was christened Edward, after his father, but his family called him by his middle name, Estlin. He was his parents' firstborn, and they expected great things from him. "I was welcomed as no son of any king and queen was ever welcomed," Cummings later wrote.

At the time of Estlin's birth, Edward Cummings taught sociology at Harvard University, which is located in Cambridge, just a short walk from Irving Street. Edward Cummings was a tall, strong man whose many talents made him seem superhuman to his son. Estlin breathlessly described his father as "a crack shot & a famous fly-fisherman & a firstrate sailor . . . & a woodsman who could find his way through forests primeval without a compass & a canoeist who'd stillpaddle you up to a deer without ruffling the surface of a pond & an ornithologist & taxidermist. . . ."

Edward Cummings knew how to design and build houses, install plumbing, take photographs, and paint pictures. He was a true optimist who liked to repeat cheerful maxims. "Anything worth doing at all is worth doing well," he often said; "smile before breakfast and shine inside." In 1900, Edward Cummings left Harvard to become a Unitarian minister at the South Congregational Church, in nearby Boston.

Estlin said that his mother, Rebecca Clarke Cummings, was "the most amazing person I've ever met." Rebecca Cummings was small and plump and wore plain, practical clothes. It was her inner qualities, and not her appearance, that most impressed her son. Loving to her family, friendly and kind to everyone, Rebecca Cummings devoted herself to her children's care. "Never have I encountered anyone more joyous, anyone healthier in body and mind, anyone quite so incapable of remembering a wrong, or anyone so completely and humanly and unaffectedly generous," Cummings said.

"Mother knew how to enjoy people and always trusted them and saw the best in them," noted Cummings's sister, Elizabeth. "She seemed to understand how people really felt about things and could always tell a big important thing from a little one, and she could see the fun in things even when the joke was on her." The children's mother had no knack for cooking, cleaning, or household repairs. She left those tasks to the family's two live-in servants and to Sandy Hardy, the African-American handyman who worked for the family by day.

Rebecca Cummings loved poetry and copied her favorite verses into a small notebook that was never out of reach. She was her children's first teacher and read to them as soon as they were old enough to understand the stories in books. When Estlin was five years old and learning to write, his mother helped him keep a diary.

Cambridge had been home to two of the most popular American poets of the

Estlin with his father and sister, Elizabeth.

The Cambridge poet James Russell Lowell
appears to be searching for the right word.

nineteenth century, Henry Wadsworth Longfellow and James Russell Lowell. Longfellow is remembered most for his poems based on American themes, including "Paul Revere's Ride" and the long narrative *The Song of Hiawatha.* Lowell's best-known work is *The Vision of Sir Launfal,* the tale of an arrogant knight searching for the Holy Grail in the days of King Arthur. Longfellow and Lowell were known as "Fireside Poets," because reading their words aloud beside a glowing hearth was a favorite American pastime. The public loved the pleasing rhymes and soothing cadences in lines such as these by Lowell:

> And what is so rare as a day in June?
> Then, if ever, come perfect days;
> Then Heaven tries the earth if it be in tune,
> And over it softly her warm ear lays. . . .

Poetry was meant "to stimulate the higher and nobler instincts which belong to the spiritual rather than to the animal nature of man," stated the introduction to a students' edition of *The Vision of Sir Launfal* that was published in 1910.

Dreaming that Estlin might grow up to be the next great Cambridge poet, Rebecca Cummings jotted down the rhymes he invented in another notebook and encouraged him to write more. According to the record she kept, Estlin recited his first original poem when he was three years old:

> Oh my little birdie oh
> With his little toe, toe, toe!

E. E. Cummings once said, "I did not decide to become a poet—I was always writing poetry."

From time to time, the Cummings home housed relatives and close friends, including the children's grandmother, Lucretia Cummings, who taught Estlin and Elizabeth to play the piano. Lucretia Cummings watched over the household like a mother hen and frequently told visitors, "I never rest easy until they are all safely in bed." Rebecca Cummings's childhood friend Emma Hathaway was a frequent guest; the children's aunt and uncle Jane Cummings and George Clarke came to stay as well. Uncle George was a lawyer with a quick wit and a happy nature that had earned him many friends.

A portrait of Rebecca Cummings in 1892, two years before Estlin was born, by Charles Sydney Hopkinson.

Talkative Estlin entertained at family dinners with lively accounts of the day's activities. Everyone laughed when he mimicked the people he had encountered. "My brother was great fun to be with," Elizabeth said. "He could draw pictures, and tell stories, and imitate people and animals, and invent games, and could make you laugh, even when you thought you felt very miserable."

In the evening, the family gathered in the parlor. Sometimes Aunt Jane or Aunt

Emma played the piano and sang. On other nights, Rebecca or Jane Cummings read aloud from classic novels such as *Treasure Island, 20,000 Leagues Under the Sea,* and *The Old Curiosity Shop.* The family particularly enjoyed a book on the Tower of London, the nine-hundred-year-old site of tortures, executions, and murders. Eager to hear the next chapter of this book, George Clarke would wait until the dinner dishes were cleared away to make this request: "Jane, let's have some ruddy gore!"

On Sundays, the family drove into Boston, where the children sat through long services at their father's church. If they kept quiet, they were permitted to ride the streetcar home to Cambridge by themselves and drink lemon phosphates at the drugstore.

In late spring, when the circus came to town, Estlin's uncle George took him to the show. Estlin Cummings grew up in the golden age of American circuses, when traveling shows tried to outdo one another at bringing thrills and glitter to towns large and small. In crowded circus big tops, Estlin marveled at clowns, trapeze artists, and daredevils such as Diavolo, who performed aerial loops on a bicycle. He was on the edge of his seat when roaring lions, lumbering elephants, and other wild animals entered the ring.

At home, Estlin played at being a circus performer. His childhood friend Betty Thaxter Hubbard recalled, "I spent most of my time watching Estlin Cummings's feats of daring in swinging and jumping from the high branches in his apple trees.

A poster advertising the Adam Forepaugh and Sells Brothers Circus, one of the thrilling big-top shows that traveled to Cambridge and other towns in the early twentieth century.

A group picture taken outside the barn at Joy Farm, about 1904. Estlin is on horseback, and Elizabeth rides the donkey. Rebecca Cummings, dressed in white, stands beside Estlin, as handyman Sandy Hardy leads the cows and a maid holds Rex, the family dog.

. . . He planned to be in a circus, and I was to be his wife and mend his clothes."

Estlin spent so much time in trees that his father built him a tree house, complete with a porch and railing and a child's bunk. This tree house quickly became a popular gathering place for the children of Irving Street, who cooked popcorn, toast, and cocoa on its miniature stove.

"My father liked to have us play in our yard and used to say he was raising children and not grass," said Elizabeth Cummings. The busy minister often worked at home in his study. "He said that happy noises, even loud ones, never disturbed him," Elizabeth added.

In 1899, the year Estlin turned five, his parents purchased Joy Farm, a working farm with a hundred-year-old farmhouse in the White Mountains of New Hampshire. Estlin was never happier than when he was chasing butterflies through the pastures of Joy Farm or exploring the woods with the family's bull terrier, Rex. His meandering eventually led him to the barn that housed a horse named Thomas à Kempis, a goat named Nan that pulled a cart, and a donkey

As a child, Estlin drew
this elephant for his father.

named Jack that gave the children rides.

At home in Cambridge at summer's end, Estlin drew pictures of farm and circus animals, especially his favorites, the elephants. He drew many other things as well: speeding trains, ships at sea, and soldiers in battle. He drew the heroes who captured his imagination, men like Buffalo Bill Cody, a colorful figure of the American West. Cody had been a trapper, a scout, and a soldier in the Indian Wars. In 1883, he became a showman, and his Wild West Show brought the expert riding, sharpshooting, and excitement of the frontier to people living east of the Mississippi River in quiet, restrained places such as Cambridge.

Cambridge was indeed a sober spot. On May 1, 1897, when Estlin Cummings was three years old, the city held its No-License Jubilee, a celebration of "ten years without the curse of an open saloon." Concerned that "disorder was on the increase in our streets" and that drinking establishments were to blame, voters had elected to outlaw saloons within city limits, beginning in 1887.

The people of Cambridge viewed their city as a tolerant place where "Catholics have come to love Protestants, and Protestants to love Catholics," said a local minister, the Reverend David Nelson Beach. Lists of houses of worship in late-nineteenth-century Cambridge are limited to Protestant and Roman Catholic churches, but Beach extended the tolerance to include nonbelievers. Furthermore, he praised the sense of community shared by the people of Cambridge proper and the residents of outlying neighborhoods such as Cambridgeport, where African Americans and immigrants from Greece, Lithuania, Armenia, and Poland were settling.

A town of poets and professors, Cambridge was proud of its history. The first printing press in America began operating in Cambridge in 1638. In 1775, General George Washington took command of the revolutionary forces under a Cambridge tree that came to be known as the Washington Elm. Its sturdy branches still offered shade more than one hundred years later, when Estlin Cummings was growing up.

Cambridge took pride as well in its fine schools. The Cummings children began their formal education at Miss Webster's School, a private institution for small boys and girls. In 1904, Estlin enrolled in the Agassiz Public School, named for the famous natural scientist Louis Agassiz, who taught at Harvard for many years. Estlin was nine years old and small for his age, but his reading skills were quite advanced. The school's African-American principal, Maria Baldwin, placed him in the seventh grade. On October 28, 1904, Baldwin commented that Estlin "is a most loveable little boy and we are glad that he is part of our little community."

The pupils had to memorize a different poem each week. Many of these were works by New England writers, such as "The Concord Hymn," Ralph Waldo Emerson's tribute to the patriots who died in the Revolutionary War battle at Concord, Massachusetts, on April 19, 1775. Emerson's poem begins:

> By the rude bridge that arched the flood,
> Their flag to April's breeze unfurled,
> Here once the embattled farmers stood,
> And fired the shot heard round the world. . . .

A horse-drawn wagon passes under the branches of the Washington Elm sometime early in the twentieth century.

In 1907, Estlin Cummings joined the freshman class at the Cambridge Latin School, a high school that prepared young people for college. There, students received a traditional nineteenth-century education, with courses in classical and modern languages, the history of the ancient world, and mathematics. Estlin studied French, Latin, and the Greek of Homer and Plato. Students mastered Latin and classical Greek by translating passages of epic works into English. Estlin especially liked studying Greek, because a lively teacher brought the old language to life. Cecil T. Derry was a young man just beginning his career. His love for his subject was contagious, and he soon had Estlin writing his translations in verse form.

Estlin was still younger and smaller than most of his classmates and shied away from sports. One student joked, "God forgive us for our short Cummings." In his free time, Estlin wrote poems inspired by religious faith, nature, and the changing seasons. He tried to sound like the New England poets on whose verses he had been raised. In "The Great White Sleep," a 1909 poem about a snowstorm, he wrote,

> The dying embers of the fire glow,
> The darkness veils the silent world outside,
> The clouded air is full of falling snow,
> And it is Christmas night. . . .

A hopeful Estlin mailed his poems to the *Atlantic Monthly, The Youth's Companion,* and other popular magazines, but the editors always rejected his work. He had better luck with the *Cambridge Review,* the monthly journal published by the city's high school students, which regularly printed his poems, stories, and essays. In his senior year, Estlin wrote a story titled "Blind," about a poet who loses his sight and learns to express himself through music. "Blind" appeared in the *Cambridge Review* and received second prize in the journal's yearly fiction contest.

Around 1909, Estlin's uncle George gave him *The Rhymester,* a handbook for writing verse. This small book examined various aspects of poems, including meter, or rhythm; devices such as simile and metaphor; and, of course, rhyme. It cautioned that a poet "must never write a line which will not sooner or later in the stanza have a line to correspond with a rhyme." In addition, he or she "must use such rhymes only as are perfect to the ear, when correctly pronounced."

"The poet gives to the world in his sublime thoughts diamonds of the purest water," the author of *The Rhymester* wrote. Estlin labored to make his own verses fit the rules set forth in this book, to make them sparkle like diamonds or pristine water.

At the same time, he delighted in writers who broke rules. One such person was George Herriman, creator of Estlin's favorite comic strip, *Krazy Kat*. Herriman wrote poems that had nothing to do with high and noble instincts, such as this one:

> T'was a long time ago I remember it well—
> A maid all alone in a poor house did dwell
> A lone with her mother, and father serene
> Her age it was red and her hair was 16. . . .

In summer, Estlin disappeared into the New Hampshire woods or perched atop a boulder and spent hours writing poetry. He wrote dozens of poems, often

The Cambridge Latin School, where Estlin attended high school.

with Rex at his side. In 1910, Estlin's father arranged for tenants to live at Joy Farm, and he built a new summer home for his family on the shore of New Hampshire's Silver Lake. Edward Cummings was always building or repairing something, and the sound of him stacking lumber or hammering nails rang through the woods. As soon as he finished the lakeshore house, he built a small shelter in the trees for Estlin, giving his son a private retreat for writing.

When the afternoons grew hot, Estlin and Elizabeth cooled off by swimming or boating on Silver Lake. One day in 1910, when Estlin was sixteen and Elizabeth was ten, they took Rex out in a canoe. The children sat on boxes, and Rex rode with his nose in the air, savoring the breeze. It was a peaceful outing until Rex snapped at a hornet that flew too close. The sudden motion upset the canoe, and suddenly Estlin, Elizabeth, and Rex were in the water. The canoe—and the life preserver it held—quickly sank.

Too far out to swim to shore, the children held on to the floating wooden boxes that had been their seats. Rex swam away, but soon, confused and tired, he returned to where the children bobbed in the water. Desperate to stay afloat, Rex climbed onto Elizabeth, pushing her underwater. Elizabeth managed to free herself and come up for air, but immediately Rex was on her again. Estlin pushed Rex away from his sister, but then the terrified dog tried to climb on him. Estlin wrestled with Rex and at last was forced to drown his beloved companion. It was the only way he and Elizabeth could survive.

A lucky coincidence saved the children. Edward Cummings had taken some of the family for a motorboat ride and happened to spot two distant figures in the water. He brought the boat closer and received a shock when he saw his wet, weary son and daughter. He wasted no time in pulling them to safety.

Rex's body floated ashore. The family gave him a ceremonial burial, and Estlin wrote a poem in tribute to his friend:

> . . . you have given your silent best,
> With silent cheerfulness to me,
> And now that our great mother
> Holds your poor body to her breast
> I come to give you my best, you see. . . .

Edward Cummings brought the boxes that had saved his children back to the house. "I keep them to remind me whenever things seem to me to be too bad," he said. Estlin's sorrow eased as life moved forward, but he never forgot Rex.

Tragedies large and small dispel the innocence of childhood. Estlin's ability to make a tough decision in an emergency and save his sister and himself signaled that his carefree boyhood was drawing to a close. He graduated from high school in the spring of 1911 and entered Harvard University that fall.

(2)

An Unknowable Bird

Harvard, the oldest college in the nation and one of the most prestigious, attracted young men from throughout the United States and from Europe, Asia, and the Middle East. (Young women attended an affiliated school, Radcliffe College.) "Harvard University undertakes to prepare young men for all the professions, including . . . all the new scientific professions, and all the higher walks of business," said Charles W. Eliot, who was president of Harvard from 1869 to 1909. "It maintains courses of instruction both elementary and advanced in all subjects of learning, both in subjects for which there is an active demand, and in those which interest but few students." The man who was president of Harvard while Estlin studied there, Abbott Lawrence Lowell, was a distant cousin of the poet James Russell Lowell.

Students at Harvard gazed at the planets from the university's observatory and learned about natural history and bygone civilizations in its several museums. They carried out experiments in its laboratories and drew knowledge from its great collection of books. At Harvard, Estlin continued his studies of ancient and modern languages. He also had classes in the sciences and economics, but he liked these less.

Estlin had the chance to study with world-renowned scholars like George Lyman Kittredge, one of the foremost authorities on Shakespeare. Kittredge demanded his students' full attention. He permitted no one to come to class late, and he forbade coughing and yawning during his lectures. He was a tall man with piercing blue eyes and a rosy face, whose hair and beard had turned white early in life. The students compared him to Santa Claus or a Viking, and they whispered

Members of the Harvard class of 1915 attend their Freshman Dinner. Estlin is among the many young men in attendance.

A Harvard student named Francis C. Walker drew this picture of George Lyman Kittredge during the 1909–10 school year. Walker was one of several students who met twice a week at Kittredge's home to discuss medieval literature. One day, the students arrived just as Kittredge learned that an old friend had died. Walker made this sketch while Kittredge reminisced about his friend. Walker, a citizen of Canada, served in the Canadian armed forces during World War I and was killed in action.

that he washed his beard in milk or powdered it with chalk. Kittredge's knowledge seemed limitless, and he answered difficult questions with ease, never once referring to books or notes.

Estlin Cummings was seventeen, young for a college freshman, and still small in stature. Although his father was over six feet tall, Estlin would only reach a height of five feet eight and one-half inches. He was a fair-haired young man with hazel eyes and a thin nose who was so self-conscious about his acne that he hid his face behind a newspaper when riding on streetcars. He lived at home rather than in a dormitory and participated in none of the clubs or fraternities that many students joined.

His first friend at Harvard was one of his teachers, Theodore "Dory" Miller, who instructed him in Greek. Miller was still young himself, just seven years older than Cummings. He taught undergraduate classes while he studied for an advanced degree. A lover of poetry, Miller aroused Estlin's interest in the great poets of ancient Greece. He also broadened his young student's knowledge of poetry written in English. Miller called the Fireside Poets boring and advised

Harvard and Cambridge in the early 1900s.

Estlin to read the leading English poets of the nineteenth century, people like Percy Bysshe Shelley, John Keats, and Alfred, Lord Tennyson.

Estlin devoured works by all of them, but he especially savored Keats. In his brief life, Keats had created some of the most beautiful poetry in the English language. His images appeal to all the senses, making it seem to readers that they not only see but also taste, hear, feel, and smell what a poem describes. Estlin paid close attention to how Keats constructed his poetry and to the way he used vowels to make his verses sound beautiful when read aloud.

In these lines from "Lamia," a poem by Keats featuring characters from Greek mythology, the *O*s ring like silver bells:

> I saw thee sitting, on a throne of gold,
> Among the Gods, upon Olympus old,
> The only sad one; for thou didst not hear
> The soft, lute-fingered Muses chanting clear,
> Nor even Apollo when he sang alone,
> Deaf to his throbbing throat's long, long melodious moan.

Throughout the school year, Miller and Cummings discussed poetry over meals of Greek and Lebanese food in Boston restaurants. In summer, they carried on their conversations at Silver Lake as they swam, hiked in the woods, and sketched the water and surrounding mountains. Cummings was writing poems about love and the natural world. In one, he described a woman coming to meet him at night: "Over

the silver meadows / Of flower-folded grass, . . . / Her feet like arrows of moonlight."

He had never had a girlfriend, but he wrote about longing for his love:

> I miss you in the dawn, of gradual flowering lights
> And prayer-pale stars that pass to drowsing-incensed hymns,
> When early earth through all her greenly sleeping limbs
> Puts on the exquisite gold day.

Late in his freshman year, Cummings began to publish his poems in the university's two literary magazines, the *Harvard Monthly* and the *Harvard Advocate*. Through these magazines, he made a few friends. One was S. Foster Damon, a handsome young man from Newton, Massachusetts, who wrote poetry and edited the *Harvard Monthly*. Damon was excited by the avant-garde and took Cummings to the International Exhibition of Modern Art when it came to Boston in 1913. Better known as the Armory Show (because it opened in the Sixty-ninth Regiment Armory in New York City), this traveling exhibition was a key event in the history of American art. It included about 1,250 works by more than three hundred European and American painters and sculptors. Many of the artists are still well known today, including the French painters Paul Gauguin and Henri Matisse, and the American James McNeill Whistler.

Some of the new art was startlingly different from anything that had been done before, and the public did not know what to make of it. Only recently had many artists stopped painting realistically and started producing abstract works. One of

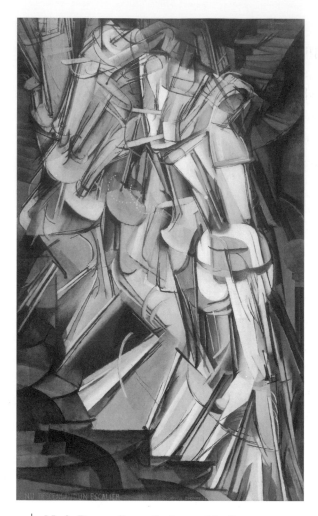

Nude Descending a Staircase, No. 2, the painting by Marcel Duchamp that created a sensation at the 1913 Armory Show.

the most important artistic movements of the early twentieth century, cubism, was an effort to present a subject from several different viewpoints at once, on a single canvas. The cubist painting *Nude Descending a Staircase, No. 2,* by Marcel Duchamp, created more controversy than anything else in the Armory Show. Duchamp had positioned one abstract human figure over another, as if to show in one picture how the complete descent of the staircase looked over time. Irate viewers compared the painting to "disused golf clubs and bags," "a dynamited suit of Japanese armor," and an "orderly heap of broken violins."

Like painters, some poets were experimenting with new effects. One daring poet was Amy Lowell, sister of Harvard's president. Amy Lowell wrote bewildering lines such as these:

> Why do the lilies goggle their tongues at me
> When I pluck them;
> And writhe and twist,
> And strangle themselves against my fingers . . .

Although she was a published poet with a growing reputation, Lowell was an embarrassment to her brother. All of Boston knew her to be an eccentric who smoked cigars and stayed up all night writing poems. It was said that she slept until three in the afternoon in an oversize bed with exactly sixteen pillows and that she had draped black cloth over the mirrors in her home.

Cummings talked about Amy Lowell with another friend, the bashful and long-legged J. Sibley Watson, who translated French verse for the *Harvard Monthly.* Sibley Watson often remained aloof—Cummings called him "mysterious"—but he was a careful observer of the world around him. Cummings also befriended Scofield Thayer, a philosophy student from a wealthy family. Thayer loved literature, the theater, painting, and sculpture. "He lived for the honor of art," Cummings said. Thayer was hard to miss: his black hair and flashing dark eyes contrasted sharply with his pale skin, and he was always neatly dressed. Other new friends were Arthur "Tex" Wilson, an aspiring painter and writer from Junction, Texas; the clever Stewart Mitchell, who was nicknamed "the Great Auk" because of his long, birdlike face; and John Dos Passos, another hopeful writer, who was nearsighted and thin as a fishing pole.

"Officially, Harvard presented me with a smattering of languages and sciences," Cummings said. "Unofficially, she gave me my first taste of independence: and the truest friends that any man will ever enjoy." Estlin took a step toward independence in his senior year, when his father permitted him to move into one of the dormitories surrounding Harvard Yard. This grassy square, crisscrossed by footpaths, is the oldest part of the Harvard campus. Estlin decorated his dormitory room with some of his favorite items, including ceramic elephants and *Krazy Kat* comic strips.

Duchamp's painting was widely parodied, as in this political cartoon titled *The Rude Descending on Sulzer.* The cartoon comments on the impeachment of New York governor William Sulzer in October 1913.

Now, with Tex Wilson, Foster Damon, and other companions, he explored Boston after dark. The young men attended plays, concerts, ballets, and operas and ate afterward in Chinese and Greek restaurants. They ventured into Scollay Square, with its dime museums and burlesque shows. At Austin and Stone's Museum, they saw people exhibited as freaks because they were too tall, too little, or too hairy, or because they had been born albino, without arms, or with deformed hands. Estlin and his friends paid ten cents admission to a popular burlesque theater, the Old Howard, to laugh at comedians' routines, watch chorus girls shimmy in short skirts, and see novelty acts like Freddy James, the Worst Juggler in the World.

Small achievements like making friends and living away from home build confidence. Socially, Estlin was coming into his own. He and his chums took young women to nightspots where musicians played ragtime music. They danced the popular turkey trot, flapping their arms, rising on the balls of their feet, and then

Estlin Cummings's senior portrait, 1915.

Young women of the burlesque theater, photographed in 1916.

dropping back to their heels. Buoyed by youth and freedom, they drove fast and recklessly in cars. One night, when Estlin went with Tex Wilson to visit a woman with a bad reputation, he parked his father's Ford in an illegal spot outside her apartment. The police sounded the Ford's horn to summon the owner, but when no one appeared, they towed it away. The car had clergyman's license plates, and when Estlin retrieved it the next morning, he brazenly pretended to be a minister and said he had been on a call of mercy, visiting a sick friend. The Reverend Cummings learned of this episode and was not amused.

In boyhood, Estlin had loved his father "with the love which is worship," he said. But now he loved him "with the love that gives battle" and saw only his faults. Edward Cummings appeared hopelessly old-fashioned to his youthful son. Estlin cringed whenever his father said, "Anything worth doing at all is worth doing well," or repeated another of his favorite sayings. He hated it that his father talked to him like a child, constantly telling him what to do and how to behave. Estlin, meanwhile, seemed to do things just to get on his father's nerves. He stopped going to church, walked around in dirty clothes and scuffed shoes, and shaved only occasionally. He laughed at his parents' advice to put on long underwear on cold days, and the underclothes he did wear were old and torn. His mother warned that he might be embarrassed if an accident landed him in the hospital, but Estlin paid no attention.

More important than the outer changes, though, were the inner ones. Estlin was becoming a man and gathering experiences and impressions to use in his poetry. A line from a letter by John Keats lingered in his mind: "I am certain of nothing but of the holiness of the Heart's affections, and the truth of the Imagination." Cummings said that when he first read this sentence, within him "an unknown and unknowable bird began singing." Keats had given him words to live by. For the rest of his life, he would follow his heart and trust his creative power.

In his senior year, Cummings signed up for advanced composition, a course with another legendary professor, Le Baron Briggs. the boyish, energetic Dean Briggs ran up staircases two and three steps at a time. He was one of the best-loved teachers at Harvard and was in his office early every morning to talk with his students or help with their problems. Briggs was a kindhearted man who rode in the baggage car on summer train trips so his dog would have company. "No one could help being moved by his lovely candor, his tenderhearted irony, the salty smalltown way he had of putting things," said Estlin's friend John Dos Passos.

Students took advanced composition in order to become better writers, and Briggs believed that the only way for them to improve was through practice. The students practiced so much that sometimes their wrists ached from writing. They prepared essays for each class on topics they chose themselves, and they wrote eight long papers throughout the semester. Briggs gave them encouragement and advice about making their writing clearer, more precise, and less wordy. "He had an old-fashioned schoolmaster's concern for the neatness of the language," Dos Passos said, "and a sharp nose for sham and pretense that was neither old nor newfashioned but eternally to the point."

One of Estlin's long papers was a commentary on "The New Art." In this paper, Cummings traced the changes that had occurred in painting and sculpture from the middle of the nineteenth century, when artists produced realistic images, through his own time, when Marcel Duchamp and others were experimenting with cubism. He wrote about the risks composers were taking in writing jarring, discordant music, and he discussed innovations in poetry. It was easy for Bostonians to laugh at this new art, Cummings wrote, but to an unbiased critic, it was "a courageous and genuine exploration of untrodden ways."

Cummings was so proud of what he'd written that when the senior class held a contest for a "commencement part," a paper to be read at graduation, he submitted a shortened version. The paper was selected, and on commencement day, June 24, 1915, Estlin Cummings stood in Harvard's Sanders Theatre with head held high, before a gathering of parents, faculty, and new graduates, to talk about "The New Art."

The listeners tried to look interested while the nervous young man lectured about painting and music, but like the majority of Americans, most thought a painting should look like something real and music should have a melody. When the speaker turned to poetry and recited "Grotesque," Amy Lowell's odd poem about lilies, some people in the audience began to hiss. Foster Damon heard one old woman say, "Is that our president's sister's poetry he is quoting? . . . Well, *I* think it is an *insult* to our president!"

"Meanwhile," said Damon, "the president's face, on which all eyes were fixed, was absolutely unperturbed." If Abbott Lawrence Lowell felt insulted, he was not about to let it show.

Cummings read another poem by Amy Lowell, "The Letter," which begins, "Little cramped words scrawling all over the paper / Like draggled fly's legs. . . ." He called this poem "superb of its kind. I know of no image in realistic writing which can approach the absolute vividness of the first two lines."

He went on to talk about Gertrude Stein, a writer who made even bolder word experiments. To Stein, the meaning of a word was less important than the beauty of the word itself. Cummings called her work "sound painting," and read a passage from her book *Tender Buttons* that included these lines:

> Elephants beaten with candy and little pops and chews all bolts and
> reckless, reckless rats, this is this. . . .
> Go red, go red, laugh white.
> Suppose a collapse is rubbed purr, is rubbed purget.
> Little sales ladies little sales ladies
> Little saddles of mutton.
> Little sales of leather and such a beautiful, beautiful, beautiful beautiful.

Now the audience laughed out loud. Cummings asked, "How much of all this is really Art? The answer is: we do not know." But, he said, "The great men of the future will certainly profit by the experimentation of the present period."

(3)

High and Clear Adventure

ummings graduated with honors that day, receiving a degree in "Literature especially in Greek and English." He then spent a fifth year at Harvard, to earn a master's degree in English, and took another course with Dean Briggs, one called English Versification.

In this course, Briggs covered the history and techniques of writing poetry in English. He followed the same formula as in his composition class, having the students write on their own time and discuss their work in class. In their writing assignments, the students practiced the different forms and styles that poets have used over the centuries. They created four-line stanzas, fourteen-line sonnets, and longer pieces. They worked to master the meters, or rhythms, that made great poems sing. They also experimented with rhymes, alliteration (repetition of letters or sounds), and similes and metaphors.

When it came to poetry, Briggs held with tradition. The way modern poets broke long-established rules made him uneasy. He was less rigid than the author of *The Rhymester,* but he taught that poets who varied line length or meter too many times, or passed off as rhymes two words that barely sounded alike, destroyed the beauty of their work. And free verse, which follows no rules whatsoever, hardly deserved to be called poetry at all, in Briggs's opinion. Class discussions turned into good-natured arguments, with Briggs and some of the students denouncing modern poetry and Cummings and the rest of the class defending it.

Estlin felt growing freedom as a poet, but he was stifled in the other aspects of his life. He was again living in the family home on Irving Street, under his parents' watchful eyes. After receiving his master's degree in 1916, he spent his days painting in the attic, trying to become an American cubist. He was tired of everything and everyone familiar: the cherubs on his bedroom wallpaper, Boston, and his father. The people of Cambridge seemed old-fashioned and narrow, and he ridiculed them in a piece of biting verse:

> the Cambridge ladies who live in furnished souls
> are unbeautiful and have comfortable minds...
> they believe in Christ and Longfellow,both dead,
> ...the Cambridge ladies do not care,above
> Cambridge if sometimes in its box of
> sky lavender and cornerless,the
> moon rattles like a fragment of angry candy

(Cummings thought that a punctuation mark alone was often enough to separate two words that were part of a single thought; punctuation and a space created too much separation.)

Dean Le Baron Briggs was often at his desk, ready to greet and counsel students.

Estlin Cummings was eager for adventure. Sometimes, he imagined himself moving to New York City and living the free, independent life of a poet and artist. At other times, he daydreamed about joining the war that was being fought in Europe and driving a speeding ambulance for the French.

His friends from Harvard were embarking on their adult lives. Tex Wilson was already living in New York, writing and painting. Stewart Mitchell, the Great Auk, had collected some of the best poems from the *Harvard Monthly,* including several by Cummings, and was working to have them published as a book. A few of Estlin's friends were even getting married. On June 21, 1916, Scofield Thayer married a beautiful young woman named Elaine Orr. He commissioned Estlin to write an epithalamion, a poem in celebration of marriage, to mark the event. Estlin wrote a long poem—his longest ever—that was full of alliteration and the ringing Os of John Keats:

O still miraculous May!O shining girl
Of time untarnished!O small intimate
Gently primeval hands,frivolous feet
Divine!O singular and breathless pearl!
O indefinable frail ultimate pose! . . .

Thayer called the poem "really corking" and paid his friend a thousand dollars for it, a great deal of money in 1916. Estlin now could afford to move to New York, but he hesitated to go until he found a job there. It took several months, but at last he was hired by P. F. Collier, the company that published *Collier's Weekly,* a popular magazine. He was thrilled with the idea of writing for a national publication, but when he reported for work in early 1917, he learned that he would be doing something else. P. F. Collier also published books like the Harvard Classics, which were inexpensive editions of fifty great books that had been selected by Charles W. Eliot, the former president of Harvard. Eliot believed that anyone could acquire an education from a "Five-foot Shelf of Books"—as long as it contained the right books. The Harvard Classics included masterpieces of literature, philosophy, religion, folklore, and history. Customers purchased the books by mail, and it was Cummings's job to send out their orders.

There was nothing thrilling about shipping books; in fact, it was deadening. To Estlin the job amounted to "warming a wooden chair for 3 and 4 hour intervals." When no one was looking, he read the newspaper or wrote poems. One day, he read in the *New York Sun* that William F. Cody, the Buffalo Bill he had admired as a child, had died. He picked up a pencil, and across a sheet of P. F. Collier stationery on which he had already jotted some notes, he wrote, "Buffalo Bill is Dead." He remembered Cody's long, flowing hair and silvery white horse. He recalled that Cody was a crack shot who could aim a rifle at clay pigeons fired into the sky and shatter them—*bang, bang, bang*—one right after another.

Later, he worked these images into a piece of free verse constructed to sound like the speech of someone who had seen Cody perform. He inserted long pauses and ran words together, just as a person's speech might hesitate and then speed up:

> Buffalo Bill's
> defunct
>   who used to
>   ride a watersmooth-silver
>   stallion
> and break onetwothreefourfive pigeonsjustlikethat
>   Jesus
>
> he was a handsome man
>   and what i want to know is
> how do you like your blueeyed boy
> Mister Death

Cummings ended his poem with an angry question that turned this simple remembrance into a comment on the cruelty of death, which steals beauty and talent from the world.

In New York, Cummings and Tex Wilson shared a sunny studio apartment with high ceilings in Greenwich Village, the Lower Manhattan neighborhood that was home to Italian immigrants and a growing number of writers and artists. Estlin found some new friends in this artistic community, among them the sculptor Gaston Lachaise. Lachaise, who had been born in France and was more than a decade older than Cummings, carved round, voluptuous female figures that were remarkable for their grace.

The narrow, angled streets of Greenwich Village were dominated by the great marble arch of Washington Square. The arch had been built in 1890 with funds collected from the public to commemorate President George Washington. Meals were cheap in the village's many small restaurants, where the talk flowed as freely as the red wine. "We were young, we were poor, and we were ambitious," said the poet Allen Tate, who knew Cummings. "We thought that the older generation was pretty bad, and we were later going to replace them."

"You hear eager discussion of everything on earth or below or above the earth," remarked a travel writer of the village in 1917. "You will suddenly hear a young

The birth of a poem: the sheet of P. F. Collier & Son stationery on which Cummings wrote "Buffalo Bill is Dead."

"Buffalo Bill" Cody, photographed in 1903. At the time, Cody was performing in London with his Wild West Show.

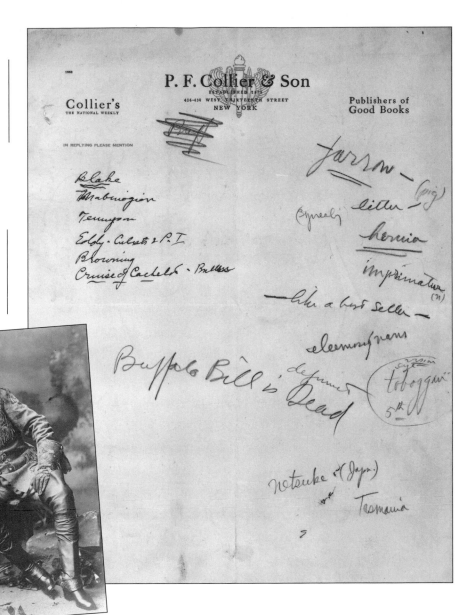

man declaim his own verses, passionately, to his young companions." That young man might have been Estlin Cummings.

By February 25, the free-spirited Cummings could no longer tolerate the P. F. Collier mailroom. Deciding he had enough money to support a simple life, he quit his job just two weeks after he started it. "I can't express to you how excellent a thing it is to be my own master (instead of the alarm clock's servant)," he wrote to his parents. The Reverend Cummings worried that Estlin was wasting his Harvard education and pursuing childish dreams. Would he ever grow up?

Estlin gloried in his freedom as he walked the length of busy Fifth Avenue.

From Washington Square he tramped north to Madison Square, where soapbox orators shouted about what was wrong with society, the government, and the world. A few blocks farther and Estlin was among the throng gazing into the windows of Lord & Taylor, Tiffany & Co., and the other great stores of the shopping district. Between Fortieth and Forty-second streets, he passed the New York Public Library, completed in 1911, its entrance guarded by majestic stone lions. Beyond were the mansions of the Vanderbilts and other wealthy families, the grand Plaza Hotel, and the landscaped hills of Central Park.

"In New York I also breathed," Cummings said, "as if for the first time." With John Dos Passos he ate baba gannouj, a roasted eggplant dish, at Khoury's Middle Eastern restaurant or walked to the aquarium at Battery Park, at the southern tip of Manhattan, to sketch the sea lions. The nervousness of adolescence had vanished, and Cummings was again a confident performer. He talked about art and poetry with friends and strangers alike at the many parties he attended and was the same entertaining speaker he had been at the dining-room table in Cambridge. "Cummings would deliver himself of geysers of talk. I've never heard anything that remotely approached it. It was comical ironical learned brilliantly colored," wrote Dos Passos. "None of us wanted to waste time at the theater when there was a chance that Cummings might go off like a stack of Roman candles after dinner!"

Increasingly, the conversation turned to world events and the war in Europe. For decades, Europe had been a smoldering continent of shifting alliances and

The Washington Square Arch, the most famous landmark in Greenwich Village. The view is looking north, up Fifth Avenue.

growing military strength, where small cultural groups, each with its own language and ancestral homeland, yearned for independence. One such place was Bosnia, on the Adriatic Sea. The Austro-Hungarian Empire had taken possession of Bosnia in 1908. The kingdom of Serbia, which was no friend of Austria-Hungary because of an economic dispute that began in 1906, supported Bosnian freedom. On June 28, 1914, Archduke Franz Ferdinand, heir to the Austrian throne, was shot and killed in Bosnia by a Serbian assassin. This event ignited a war between Austria-Hungary and Serbia that quickly spread. By August, nations had chosen sides, and much of Europe was at war. Austria-Hungary, Germany, Turkey, and Bulgaria—the Central Powers—opposed Serbia, France, Great Britain, Russia, and Belgium—the Allies.

The United States had a policy of neutrality, but in January 1917, Germany threatened to use "every available weapon" to stop all sea traffic to and from Great Britain, and it looked as though the United States might be forced to enter the war. The future appeared increasingly grim as Germany carried out its threat. In February, March, and April, Germans submarines sank a thousand ships of all classes. In one two-week period in April, Allied and neutral nations lost one hundred twenty-two ocean-going vessels. Ships were sinking twice as fast as they could be built.

Could the United States afford to do nothing? Many Americans were eager to join the fight, while others objected to such a radical change in policy. American socialists opposed a war that in their view would be fought to protect the shipping industry. Some African Americans declared that it was wrong to fight for freedom in other lands while their own race was denied freedom at home. The Reverend Cummings headed the World Peace Foundation, an organization that studied ways to prevent wars and keep the world at peace. This and similar groups saw international conflicts as social problems requiring reasoned solutions, not guns. Estlin was less interested in world affairs than his father and many others were, but he, too, favored peace. He would never understand war.

On April 6, 1917, the United States declared war against Germany. The next day, Estlin joined the Norton-Harjes Ambulance Service, a Red Cross unit that was aiding the French army. He knew that if he waited, he would be drafted into the U.S. armed forces. Ambulance service offered a way to get close to the action but remain at a fairly safe distance from the battle lines. It appealed to pacifists, because by driving and repairing ambulances, they could experience the war, one

A panorama of Paris.

of the most significant events of their lifetime, without having to pick up a weapon.

(It should be noted that the majority of Americans supported the war and that 4,355,000 men and women of all races served in the U.S. mobilized forces during World War I. The voices of protest were drowned by the noise of patriotic rallies or silenced by the Sedition Act of 1918, a federal law that made it a crime to speak out against the government or the military.)

On April 28, Estlin sailed for Europe aboard the *Touraine,* a French ocean liner. Standing at the rail, he waved to his mother, who had traveled from Cambridge to see him off, and to the friends who had come to the pier to wish him well.

Just after sailing out of sight of land, the *Touraine* headed into a storm. As soon as the waves calmed down, Estlin took a stroll on the deck and spotted a face that looked slightly familiar. He introduced himself to the beefy, dark-haired fellow and learned that he was Slater Brown, whose family had lived next door to the Cummingses for a year when both young men were children. Brown, who was two years younger than Cummings, had grown up in Webster, Massachusetts, and had just graduated from Columbia University in New York City with a degree in English and French. An ardent pacifist, he had taken part in a failed movement to stop Congress from declaring war. Now, like Cummings, he was headed for France to serve with the Norton-Harjes Ambulance Corps. Small world!

By the time their ship docked in Bordeaux in early May, Estlin and Slater were close friends. They rode in a different car from the other recruits when the ambulance-corps volunteers traveled to Paris by train, and were so busy talking about poetry and art that they failed to notice when the others got off at the wrong

stop. They were surprised to be the only recruits to reach the correct station, the Gare Orléans, and dismayed to find the Norton-Harjes headquarters closed. They spent the night at a hotel and went back the next day, when the office was open. This time, the staff told them to return to their hotel, order their uniforms, and await further instructions.

Then, somehow, the Norton-Harjes Ambulance Service forgot about Estlin Cummings and Slater Brown. Each day, the young Americans expected to be told to report for duty, but each day, no instructions came. It gradually dawned on Estlin and Slater that they were on their own in Paris. Life had handed them an opportunity—and they made the most of it.

Less than a hundred miles away, Allied and German soldiers were engaged in brutal trench warfare. Germany's "scorched earth" policy had turned French villages near the Western Front to wreckage and cinders, but Paris showed few effects of the war. It remained the cultured, free and easy city it had been in pre-war years. Brown and Cummings ate lazy breakfasts at sidewalk cafés as they watched the traffic on the crowded boulevards. By day, they browsed through volumes of French poetry at the bookstalls lining the river Seine, and by night, they attended the ballet. Cummings was "the most entertaining man I ever met," Brown said. "He was a dreadful show-off. Everything he did was a performance." They saw treasures of painting and sculpture at the Louvre, Paris's great art museum, and the latest cubist works in the galleries of Montmartre. Estlin even had a brief romance with a French prostitute named Marie Louise, and Slater Brown befriended her roommate, Mimi.

Cummings called Paris a "divine section of eternity." He filled his sketchbook with drawings of women at the market, children watching sidewalk puppet shows, and soldiers and sailors on leave. "Now, finally and first, I was myself," Cummings said, "one with all human beings born and unborn."

The good times ended on June 12, when Cummings and Brown were called to Norton-Harjes headquarters by Monsieur Harjes himself and scolded for playing hooky. They were assigned to *Section Sanitaire XXI* of the ambulance service, which was stationed in the village of Ham, northeast of Paris and close to the front. In times of battle, the ambulance volunteers transported wounded French soldiers to hospitals, but the guns were quiet in their sector when Cummings and Brown arrived. The volunteers spent their days cleaning the ambulances and waiting for something to happen, and Cummings and Brown were bored. The food in camp was terrible, and they looked down on the other volunteers, who were mere "average" Americans, in Cummings's opinion. They preferred talking to the eight Frenchmen assigned to the section and any French soldiers they happened to meet.

The pair had little respect for the section chief, who chewed them out for lacking "sticktuitiveness and enthusiasm." When he denied them seven days' leave in Paris but granted it to others, Cummings had the nerve to blow cigarette smoke in his face. Such an offense would have brought swift punishment in the regular army, but chiefs in the volunteer ambulance corps lacked true military authority. Cummings's contempt for higher-ups would land him in trouble only when he angered French officials—which happened soon after this event.

In their off-duty hours, Brown and Cummings wrote letters. Cummings complained to his parents about the bad food and boredom in camp. Together, the two composed a letter to the French undersecretary of aviation and asked to join the Lafayette Esquadrille, a unit of American flyers attached to the French armed forces. The letters Brown wrote by himself to his friends and relatives at home were more serious. He passed along rumors, including the belief, held by some French soldiers, that Germany would be victorious.

Cummings and Brown liked ambulance service even less when a new section chief took charge. Harry Anderson was a mechanic from New York City who ran his corps like a military unit and was unimpressed by young men with college degrees. To him, the two volunteers from Massachusetts were unshaven troublemakers in grease-stained uniforms. Anderson was out to show off American superiority to the French, to demonstrate "how they do things in America," Cummings

American ambulance drivers in France. In May 1917, the American Red Cross became coordinator of all volunteer ambulance services in France. In August 1917, the U.S. Army took over this responsibility.

said. He told his men "to keep away from those dirty Frenchmen," but Brown and Cummings ignored his instructions. Clearly, they had attitude problems.

On Sunday, September 23, Anderson ordered Brown and Cummings to clean and grease his private vehicle. The friends had just about finished this "unlovely" job when the French minister of safety rode into camp, accompanied by soldiers and police officers. He marched over to Brown and Cummings and ordered them to collect their belongings. They were being taken to the town of Noyon for questioning. As they were packed into vehicles and driven away, Cummings was ecstatic. At last, he thought, he had found what he was looking for, "a high and clear adventure."

In Noyon, the French interrogated Brown and Cummings separately. Brown was first, and when he emerged from the minister's office, he said to his friend, "I think we're going to prison all right."

There was no time to ponder his meaning, because it was Cummings's turn to face a panel of three examiners: the minister, a man in a business suit who looked like a lawyer, and an older man who wore the Legion of Honor, a medal awarded by the French government to distinguished people from all walks of life. The panel asked Cummings about his friendship with Brown, their time in Paris, and their ambulance duty. Then the minister said, "You are aware that your friend has written to friends in America and to his family very bad letters."

"I am not," Cummings replied, but he was starting to get the picture. French censors had read Brown's letters, decided they contained dangerous opinions, and notified the authorities. The French saw Brown as a threat, and Cummings had come under suspicion because he was Brown's friend.

The panel asked Cummings about the letter he had written with Brown to the undersecretary of aviation. Did he truly want to fly? Would he drop bombs on enemy targets? But they kept returning to the subject of Brown. "We have the very best reason for supposing your friend to be no friend of France," the minister said.

As the interview was ending, the minister asked Cummings if he hated the Germans. Cummings understood that he could answer yes and walk out a free man, his loyalty a matter of public record. He refused to lie, though, and because he hated no one, he replied, "*J'aime beaucoup les français.*" ("I like the French very much.")

"It is impossible to love Frenchmen and not to hate Germans," the minister said. "I am sorry for you, but due to your friend you will be detained a little while." Cummings was conducted to a nearby prison and locked in a narrow room furnished only with a pile of straw. The next day, the French transferred the two suspects to a detention camp in the town of La Ferté-Macé, west of Paris, to await questioning by a commission that would decide their fate. They could be set free, shipped home to the United States, court-martialed, or sent to a concentration camp, depending on whether the commission thought they were innocent or guilty.

Before the first Nazi death camps became operational, in 1941, a concentration camp was a place of internment for prisoners of war or people who had aroused government suspicion. During World War I, French concentration camps housed political prisoners and German and Austrian citizens living in France who had done nothing illegal.

The detention facility at La Ferté-Macé was built entirely of gray stone. It consisted of three buildings that had been a seminary before the war, surrounded by a seven-foot wall. Cummings and Brown were confined with about forty other men in a large third-story room with a high, arched ceiling that resembled a chapel. Many of the windows had been boarded up, and pails filled to the brim with urine stood here and there.

Days passed in the routine of prison: Guards awakened the men at six-thirty each morning and marched them downstairs to the mess hall for meals. The prisoners had bread and coffee for breakfast, and bread and soup for lunch and dinner. They exercised in a courtyard for short periods every morning and evening, and they went to sleep at nine o'clock each night. The authorities allowed them to keep their money and possessions and to send and receive mail. Cummings and Brown ordered a set of Shakespeare's plays from a Paris bookstore.

Most of the other prisoners were small-time criminals from France and other countries in Europe and the Middle East. Cummings met all kinds of men who each had somehow offended the French authorities: a clean-shaven young Norwegian who spoke perfect English and had worked on a ship, shoveling coal into the furnace; a large black man named Jean, who claimed at times to be English and at other times French; a ragged figure with wisps of dirty hair whose movements reminded Cummings of a dancing bear.

Estlin Cummings, who had rejected the comradeship of Americans in the ambulance corps, rejoiced in the brotherhood of the inmates. He was seeing a new side of life, and in a letter to his mother he wrote, "I am having *the time of my life!*"

(4)

Love and Telegrams; Poems and Soldiering

Estlin's parents learned of his imprisonment before his flippant letter arrived; they had received a telegram from Paris, from Richard Norton of the Norton-Harjes Ambulance Corps: EDWARD E. CUMMINGS HAS BEEN PUT IN A CONCENTRATION CAMP AS A RESULT OF LETTERS HE HAD WRITTEN STOP AM TAKING UP THE MATTER THROUGH THE EMBASSY TO SEE WHAT CAN BE DONE.

The Reverend Cummings reacted by sending a flurry of telegrams and letters on his son's behalf. He urged Norton to keep up his appeals to the U.S. Embassy and the American Red Cross, and he counseled Estlin to be brave. "No child of your mother could ever lack courage or patriotism. You have plenty of both," he wrote. Rebecca Cummings sent her son a cable asking him to "TAKE THE GREATEST CARE FOR MY SAKE."

When Norton's efforts in Paris yielded no results, Edward Cummings sought help from his friend George W. Anderson, head of the Interstate Commerce Commission in Washington, D.C. Anderson persuaded the secretary of state to demand from the embassy in Paris a full report on prisoners Cummings and Brown. Finally, wheels began to turn—slowly.

The U.S ambassador queried the military, and on October 26, the army informed him that the French commission had questioned the two Americans. The French had decided to set Cummings free, but Brown was to be held in a concentration camp for the duration of the war. Then, on November 21, Anderson passed along to his friend in Cambridge a somber message he had received: E. E. Cummings had been aboard the transport ship *Achilles* when it was torpedoed by a German submarine on October 17 and was presumed dead.

Edward Cummings kept this distressing news from his wife, who never doubted Estlin's eventual safe return, as he investigated whether it was true. He was greatly relieved to discover, three days later, that there had been a mistake, that the name on the casualty list was H. H. Cummings. But he still had no idea what was happening to his son. Where in the world was he?

On December 8, a desperate Edward Cummings called upon President Wilson to intervene in this "crime against American citizenship in which the French government has persisted for many weeks. . . .

"I do not speak for my son alone; or for him and his friend alone," Cummings wrote. "My boy's mother had a right to be protected from the weeks of horrible anxiety and suspense caused by the inexplicable arrest and imprisonment of her son." He stated that if the situation were reversed, if he were president and Wilson's son were unjustly imprisoned, he would do everything possible to make American citizenship "sacred in the eyes of Frenchmen."

Wilson received many letters from private citizens seeking his help, but most were forwarded to other offices and never reached his desk. Whether the president

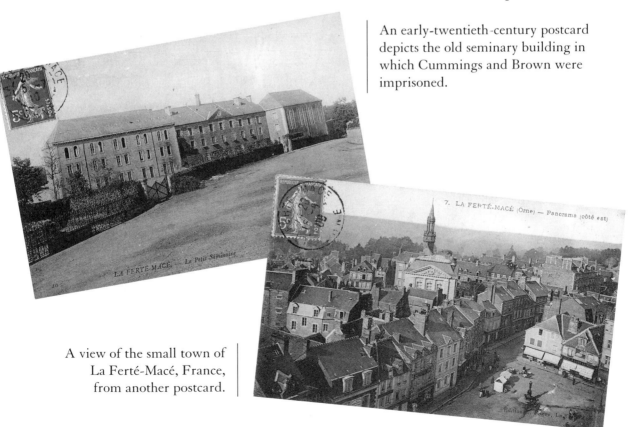

An early-twentieth-century postcard depicts the old seminary building in which Cummings and Brown were imprisoned.

A view of the small town of La Ferté-Macé, France, from another postcard.

The New York City skyline, shown here in a photograph made sometime between 1910 and 1930, was a welcome sight to a returning former prisoner.

looked into the case of Estlin Cummings and Slater Brown is unknown, but Cummings was released from the detention center at La Ferté-Macé on December 19. He traveled by train to Paris on December 20, met the American ambassador, and sailed for the United States two days later. On January 1, 1918, with grateful eyes, he saw from the ship the "impossibly tall, incomparably tall" buildings of Manhattan and heard "the noises of America," which "nearingly throbbed with smokes and hurrying dots which are men and which are women and which are things new and curious and hard and strange and vibrant and immense." He was home.

In a moment, Estlin Cummings—thin, undernourished, and with an open sore on his leg—was embracing his mother on the pier. His father arrived in New York later that day, and soon father, mother, and son headed for Cambridge, where Estlin would recuperate.

Eight Harvard Poets, the book assembled by Stewart Mitchell, had come out while Cummings was in prison. John Dos Passos's wealthy father had paid most of the publication costs, and each poet had agreed to buy thirty copies. The book contained eight poems by Cummings, four works of free verse and four sonnets. In one, Cummings wrote about a chorus girl, a "little painted poem of God," whom he perhaps had seen dancing in Scollay Square. In another, he described a garden where:

colors come and go.
Frail azures fluttering from night's outer wing,
Strong silent greens serenely lingering,
Absolute lights like baths of golden snow.

The ominous figure of death appears in the brief poem "Epitaph." As a woman with tumbling hair wanders through a field picking wildflowers, "Another comes / also picking flowers."

It angered Cummings to see that the publisher had made changes in his poetry. In the poem "Crepuscle" ["Twilight"] and elsewhere, Cummings had used a lowercase i for the first-person singular pronoun, but now it was capitalized throughout his work. This might have been a minor point to the publisher, but it was a serious matter to Cummings, who used every aspect of writing, from spacing to capitalization to punctuation (or its absence), to add meaning to his poetry. A lowercase i let readers know that the poet was referring to his private self. A capital letter might give emphasis, or it might suggest more than one way of interpreting the poet's lines.

Readers can start to grasp this richness in the poem "Finis," from *Eight Harvard Poets:*

In a golden greeting

splendidly to westward

as pale twilight

trem-

bles

into

Darkness

comes the last light's gracious exhortation. . . .

In this description of a sunset, the final rays of sunlight come as "a golden greeting," and twilight fades with a tremor into darkness. But Cummings capitalized Darkness, hinting that this word also begins a thought, if just a small one: "Darkness / comes. . . ."

Estlin was home and safe, but Edward Cummings's blood was still boiling because of the way France had dealt with his son and the way the Red Cross and

The Twelfth Infantry Division lines up at Camp Devens
for review, September 14, 1918.

the U.S. Embassy had dragged their heels. He threatened to launch an international lawsuit, to force the French government to admit to this injustice and expose this shameful treatment of a U.S. citizen to the American public. He had saved copies of all his letters and telegrams, and he now asked Estlin to write a detailed account of his prison experience.

But Estlin was dead set against any legal action. He was starting to feel better and was eager to return to his painting and poetry. To put the matter to rest, he offered to write the story of his imprisonment—if his father promised not to start a lawsuit. Edward Cummings agreed to those terms and said he would even pay Estlin for the time spent writing. This was an extraordinary offer. At the time, it was unusual for a father to pay his son for any kind of task, especially writing a book. In fact single, adult children commonly worked and gave part of their earnings to their mothers and fathers.

All too soon, to his parents' way of thinking, Estlin was making plans to get back to New York. He and his father argued about the future: Wasn't it time to stop playing with paints and grow up and get a job? Shouldn't Estlin worry that he might be drafted into the army? After all, there was still a war going on! Why didn't he volunteer for officer's training like other Harvard graduates?

Estlin would hear none of it. In February 1918, he moved into a small house in Greenwich Village, and in April, Slater Brown joined him. The French had released Brown upon the urging of Senator Henry Cabot Lodge of Massachusetts, and now Brown became part of Cummings's circle of friends in New York. He joined Estlin and the others for cheap shish-kebob dinners at Khoury's restaurant,

for stargazing from city rooftops, and for teatime gatherings at the apartment of
Elaine Thayer. The two-year-old marriage of Scofield and Elaine Thayer was
clearly failing. The couple lived apart, and Scofield spent much of his time in
Chicago, managing a literary magazine called the *Dial*.

Scofield Thayer continued to support Cummings's art. He commissioned
cubist paintings from his friend and showed his poems to the editors of the *Dial*.
Meanwhile, his lonely wife responded to Cummings's friendship, and he, in turn,
was attracted to her beauty. He reminded himself that Elaine was "Another's and
Belongs to Another Person," but the two were falling in love.

In July 1918, Cummings was drafted into the army, just as his father had feared.
He said goodbye to Elaine and his friends and reported to Camp Devens,
Massachusetts, for training. Constructed in 1917, this five-thousand-acre military
facility prepared more than one hundred thousand soldiers for service in World
War I. Cummings was assigned to Company Three, First Battalion, Depot Brigade
and trained as an infantryman, or foot soldier. Depot Brigades acted as receiving
units for men who had been drafted and trained soldiers as replacements for units
in the field.

In letters written from Camp Devens, Cummings explained to his perplexed
parents why he had let himself be drafted. It was wrong, he said, to use advantages
like his intelligence and his Harvard connections to escape the dangers less fortunate young men had to face. Also, it was his duty as an artist to see and experience
as much of life as he could. "The artist is merely the earth's most acute and wiley
observer of everything-under-the-sun," he wrote. "The artist keeps his eyes,ears,&

White soldiers lean out barracks windows to stare at black recruits who have just arrived at Camp Devens for training. American soldiers served in segregated units during World War I. In fact, the U.S. armed forces did not begin integrating until 1948.

above all his NOSE wide open,he watches,while others merely execute orders he *does things.*" Estlin reminded his parents that, like it or not, his life and his choices were his own: "Mine is the perspiration of my own existence . . . and I would not change it for anyone else's sweat under heaven."

His superiors recommended Cummings for officer training, based on his education and scores on psychological tests, but he refused it, insisting he wanted no rank or responsibility for others. Instead, he was given a noncommissioned officer's rank, acting corporal, and he did his best to be as unimportant as possible.

For someone eager to experience a soldier's life, Estlin Cummings certainly complained! He whined about all the marching, drilling, and regimentation of camp life; he griped that army food tasted like "a semi-liquid demiviscous pudding-of-rubber-heels"; he held himself apart from his fellow soldiers, who called him Eddie. But what most repelled him at Camp Devens was the constant pressure to hate the Germans. During bayonet practice, a drill instructor told him, "Stick it in the bellies,And Don't Stick It In Deep,stick it in *A Little Way. There's nothing better than to see a Bosch* [German] *die.*"

The treatment of a pacifist unlucky enough to be drafted was particularly chilling. A big, good-natured soldier, whose name Cummings forgot, willingly obeyed every order—except when his superiors ordered him to pick up a gun, because it was against his beliefs to hate and kill. The base commander called this soldier into his office and tried to talk sense into him. "What would you do if some German came through the window and raped your sister?" he asked. The soldier told Cummings that he replied with the truth: "Sir, I have no sister." The next day the gentle soldier was gone, and a rumor circulated that he had been sent to the army prison at Fort Leavenworth, Kansas. Cummings had heard that some army prison guards beat and tortured conscientious objectors.

A small number of recruits suffered abuse, but more endured illness. A deadly form of influenza that was sweeping the world reached Camp Devens in September 1918. Hundreds of men became sick and died, but Cummings escaped infection. For him, one day was just like another. Corporal Cummings spent off-duty hours in the recreation hall or at the YMCA, reading and writing letters and sending love poems to Elaine. In one, he wrote:

> my love is building a building
> around you,a frail slippery
> house,a strong fragile house . . .

Impatient for something—anything—to happen, in early fall, he requested transfer to a combat unit. He was reassigned to the Twelfth Infantry Division, but before his unit could be sent to fight, the war ended. On November 11, 1918, the victorious Allies and the defeated Central Powers signed an armistice.

The army immediately began bringing home the soldiers stationed overseas and discharging thousands of men into civilian life. This was a big task that took time. In December, the soldiers of Cummings's old unit, the Depot Brigade, received their discharge papers, but those on duty with the Twelfth Infantry at Camp Devens were assigned four more months of training. Any soldier who protested—and Cummings was one— was given KP (kitchen police, or mess-hall) duty.

Claiming his temperament made him unsuited for army life, Cummings applied for a discharge, and in

Cummings, home from Camp Devens on leave, in his army uniform.

Elaine Orr Thayer at the Thayer family's summer home in 1919.

January, he was called in to meet with the camp commander. Whether it was because he mentioned his service with the ambulance corps, or because he said that Scofield Thayer had commissioned four paintings from him and he could not fulfill the contract while in uniform, or because the commander was weary of hearing complaints, he was discharged.

He hurried back to New York, to his painting and his poetry. He finished the paintings for Thayer, filling canvases with bright colors, geometric shapes, angles, and swirls. That spring, he entered two of his paintings in the Independent Artists' Show, an annual exhibit that gave modern artists a chance to put their work before the public. Cummings described the first of these paintings, titled *Sound, Number One,* as "a lot of circles going on a bat." The other, *Noise, Number One,* he called "more swimmingish." In these works, he attempted to capture on canvas the clamor of modern life.

Cummings went often with his friends to the rooftop gallery of the Waldorf-Astoria Hotel, where the paintings were displayed, and he was overjoyed when a critic from the *New York Sun* singled out his work for praise. "The brilliant sally in color by Mr. Cummings will greatly impress those who have arrived at an appreciation of the abstract in art," the critic wrote. Soon another Cummings painting, *Noise, Number Two,* was hanging in a Greenwich Village gallery.

That spring, Cummings also thought about publishing a volume of poems. He and Slater Brown came up with possible book titles by putting together nouns that seemed to have nothing in common: "fishhooks and pajamas," "lilacs and monkey-wrenches," and "squirrels and efficiency." Cummings and Brown were sharing a studio apartment in Greenwich Village, on the fourth floor of a building with no elevator. Their studio had no running water, so they had to use a toilet and sink on the floor below and carry up buckets of water for cooking and washing. A fireplace provided the only heat.

Cummings had also come back to Elaine. Although she was the estranged wife of a friend, he found it impossible to stay away from her. Their love deepened, and in the spring, Elaine told Estlin that she was pregnant and that he was the baby's father.

This was a dilemma. For a married woman to have a child with a man other than her husband, something scandalous today, was all the more shocking in 1919. Even if Elaine were to divorce Scofield and marry Estlin, gossips would count on their fingers the months between the wedding and the baby's birth and start whispering. Both Scofield and Estlin urged Elaine to have an illegal abortion. Scofield hoped to protect the reputations of everyone involved: Elaine, Estlin, himself, and their families. To Estlin, taking on the responsibilities of husband and father felt too much like being a grownup. Besides, for an artist and poet, a family might only get in the way.

Elaine refused to have an abortion, though. She and Scofield talked the matter over and agreed that whether they stayed married or parted, they would raise the child as their own. Scofield confided to Estlin that he no longer loved Elaine. How Elaine felt about the situation is anyone's guess, but it is hard to imagine that she was happy.

That summer, while the Thayers vacationed at Scofield's mother's beach house in Edgartown, Massachusetts, Estlin went to his family's home at Silver Lake. He "withdrew from reality," he said, and "sought refuge in unreality, ideas," and art. With Elaine on his mind, he composed the long poem, "Puella Mea," which is Latin for "My Girl."

In this playful work, Cummings compares his lady to the great beauties of literature and legend, to Princess Salome of the Bible, Helen of Troy, and Guinevere of Camelot. He decides, "Lovely as those ladies were / mine is a little lovelier." He describes his lady from top to toe, starting with "The immaculate and crisp head" and moving to her "very singular and slenderest hands"; her waist, "a most tiny hinge / of flesh, a winsome thing and strange"; and her ankle, "divinely shy; / as if for fear you would espy / the little distinct foot. . . ."

Cummings ends this poem by addressing the "Eater of all things lovely—Time! / upon whose watering lips the world poises a moment . . . / gesticulates, and disappears. . . ." The mutability of life (the fleeting, temporary nature of our existence), an important theme in all of literature, had become central to Cummings's work.

Scofield Thayer, in a photograph taken around 1919.

When the world was like a song
heard behind a golden door . . .
when the world was like a tale
made of laughter and of dew . . .
softly used to wholly move
slender ladies made of dream . . .

Elaine gave birth to a girl, named Nancy Thayer, on December 20, 1919. Estlin visited mother and child and reported to his sister that "Elaine Thayer's daughter looks just like a doll—she has ever so much very long hair." He had kept the secret of his fatherhood from everyone, including his family.

Scofield Thayer remained Estlin's friend despite the adulterous affair that had resulted in Nancy's birth. The magazine Thayer edited, the *Dial,* had moved its offices to New York City during the summer of 1918, while Estlin was stationed at Camp Devens. In November 1919, Thayer and Sibley Watson had purchased the *Dial* and begun carefully building it into what would become the nation's leading journal of art and literature of the 1920s.

Thayer and Watson's first issue, published in January 1920, contained seven poems by E. E. Cummings. His verses about Buffalo Bill were there, although the exclamation "Jesus" was likely to raise eyebrows. Thayer and Watson had also selected a delicate poem about death and rebirth that Cummings had written for Dean Briggs's poetry class:

when god lets my body be

From each brave eye shall sprout a tree
fruit that dangles therefrom

the purpled world will dance upon
Between my lips which did sing

a rose shall beget the spring
that maidens whom passion wastes

will lay between their little breasts . . .

Gaston Lachaise's sculpture *The Mountain.*

The next issue of the *Dial* included an essay by Cummings on the art of his sculptor friend Gaston Lachaise. Cummings particularly praised one work, *The Mountain,* a rotund female figure seventeen inches long, lying on her side. Lachaise had not sculpted one specific woman or even tried to create a realistic woman, and to Cummings this was key. Rather than produce something copied or secondhand, Lachaise had been original. *The Mountain* was not a portrait "OF Some One" or a statue "OF something," but "a phenomenon," whose importance lay strictly in itself. To contemplate *The Mountain* was to immerse oneself in the language of stone and surface and mass. "In his enormous and exquisite way, Lachaise negates OF with IS," Cummings wrote.

"Lachaise's work is the absolutely authentic expression of a man very strangely alive."

What a necessary thing for an artist to be: *Alive.*

(5)

F i r s t n e s s

in Just-
spring   when the world is mud-
luscious the little
lame balloonman

whistles   far   and wee

and eddieandbill come
running from marbles and
piracies and it's
spring

when the world is puddle-wonderful

the queer
old balloonman whistles
far   and   wee
and bettyandisbel come dancing

from hop-scotch and jump-rope and

it's

            spring
            and

                        the

                                    goat-footed

            balloonMan   whistles
            far
            and
            wee

The May 1920 issue of the *Dial* contained five poems by E. E. Cummings in celebration of spring, including what is possibly his most famous work, the untitled
poem that begins, "in Just- / spring." Here was a poem about springtime in
Cambridge, when children, who might include Estlin and Elizabeth (eddie and
isbel), play in the puddle-rich world of Irving Street. The balloon man whistles to
the children, as he so often did when Estlin was a boy, but now he is "queer" and
"goat-footed," as though he is something more than he first appears to be. Is he
Pan, the Greek god of nature, whose form was part human and part animal? A
marvelous musician, Pan was forever playing his pipes to entrance the nymphs, the
mythical maidens of the sea and woods. The youngsters running from their games
remind us that life beckons to all children, and that we all outgrow the naïveté of
childhood and awaken sexually.

Cummings felt lucky to have "what amounts to my own printing-press in
Thayer and Watson." The publishers of the *Dial* were eager to print his poems and
paid careful attention to his innovations, like the placement of commas and quirks
of capitalization, which Cummings called "my Firstness."

That spring Cummings submitted two large paintings, *Sound, Number Five* and
Noise, Number Five to the Independent Exhibition of 1920. More than three thousand people attended the opening of this show, and spectators had to stand on tiptoe to peer over heads or push through the crowd to see the paintings. Again,
Cummings's work received critical attention. A writer for the *Globe and Commercial
Advertiser* stated that in any future exhibition of abstract art, "paintings by E. E.
Cummings should be included."

Painting and writing kept Estlin very busy. He had put aside the book he was

Men selling balloons were a common sight in American cities and towns a century ago. This balloon man plies his trade in San Francisco's Chinatown.

Men selling balloons were a common sight in American cities and towns a century ago. This balloon man plies his trade in San Francisco's Chinatown.

writing about his imprisonment in France, but he picked it up again at Silver Lake in the summer of 1920. In order to write without distractions, he pitched a tent on a point of land that was reached most easily by canoe, and lived there alone. In the evening, he paddled across the lake to join his family for dinner and collect the next day's provisions. He wrote slowly, making "every paragraph a thing which seemed good to me." He was stitching together a fabric of sentences and paragraphs that reminded him of a crazy quilt. "In every inch there is a binding rhythm which integrates the whole thing and makes it a single moving Thing InItself," he said. At summer's end, when the rest of the family left Silver Lake, Estlin stayed and kept writing, with Slater Brown keeping him company and refreshing his memory of La Ferté-Macé.

When it was almost November and the first snowflakes were falling in New Hampshire, the book was finished. At Christmas, Estlin gave his father the honor of being its first reader, and even before finishing it, Edward Cummings understood that the book was significant. He told his son, "I am sure now that you are a *great writer,* and as proud of it now, as I shall be when the world finds out."

But would the world ever discover Estlin's greatness? One publisher after another turned his book down, and he had sold paintings only to his friends. He was also trying to publish a book of poems, but he was having no luck with that project, either. Tired of feeling discouraged, on March 15, 1921, he sailed for Europe with John Dos Passos aboard a Portuguese freighter. "Dos" had already published two novels, *One Man's Initiation—1917,* based on his experiences as an ambulance driver in France, and *Three Soldiers,* an antiwar novel. Estlin told his family he'd be away for "a year or a century," and he left his father to find a publisher for his book.

The ship pitched and rolled so much that Estlin and Dos called it the "Holy Roller." They docked in Lisbon after three weeks of seasickness and wandered up the coast of Portugal before heading inland to Spain. Estlin carried a sketchpad and made pencil drawings of the people and scenes that captured his interest. He drew bathers posing on a beach, church steeples, pastures and cultivated fields, heads of goats, and the twisted branches of olive trees. Here and there, he jotted down poetic phrases that came to his mind: "a boy barefooting stolidly along / low tide, followed by his kite, / his idea. . . ."

Estlin and Dos reached Seville in April, at the time of the yearly festival. "I wish you could have seen the feria [fair]," Estlin wrote to his mother; "the streets crammed with carriages in which the most exquisite girls rode,each with her mantilla,superb scarlet and vermillion. . . . At night the various clubs gave dances in the open,in little pavilions along certain streets. Men and girls stood up with castanets,swaying,twisting,stamping;spectators seated in a ring clapped in time;there was music and often singing." In Seville, Cummings and Dos Passos attended two bullfights, and Estlin had a toothache treated by a Spanish dentist.

They toured the Prado, the famous art museum in Madrid, with its great col-

Cummings's friend
John Dos Passos,
shown here in the 1920s.

lection of European paintings. They saw the 1619 work *The Adoration of the Magi,* by Diego Velàzquez, in which the artist painted his own family as biblical figures. They also studied dark scenes of war painted in the early 1800s by another Spanish master, Francisco José de Goya. Estlin, who preferred to see modern art, thought the Prado housed too many old paintings.

The two travelers went to the Basque country of north-central Spain, where the people speak an ancient tongue unrelated to any other European language. From there, they set off to hike across the Pyrenees Mountains, never imagining they would wade through waist-deep snow or slide down so many icy inclines that Estlin would wear out the seat of his trousers. From the French side of the mountains, they caught a train that brought them to Paris by mid-May. They took a room in a cheap hotel on the Left Bank, an area where many students lived, and Estlin continued sketching and recording his impressions.

From Paris, he sent a long letter to Elizabeth, who had recently graduated from Radcliffe College. Elizabeth had complained that their father was interfering in her life. Estlin responded with advice on dealing with the Reverend Cummings and on living fully and honestly. "NEVER BE AFRAID," he counseled. "NEVER take ANYONE'S word for ANYTHING. Find out *for yourself*!!!!" He also wrote, "*There is no such thing* as 'doing wrong' or 'being right about something'—these are 4th hand absurdities invented by the aged in order to prevent the young from being alive."

Estlin reminded Elizabeth that he had progressed in his painting because he had chosen to paint in his own way, and not as others thought he should. He had gone against his father during the war, when he refused to apply for officer's training, because it was the wrong course for him. He told Elizabeth, "To Hell with everything which tries,no matter how kindly,to prevent me from LIVING MY OWN LIFE—KINDNESS,always,is MORE DANGEROUS than anything else!"

For anyone doing something new in the arts, Paris in the 1920s was Mecca. It attracted composers of discordant, modern music, including Igor Stravinsky, a

Russian, and Virgil Thomson, an American. Writers, from the Americans Gertrude Stein and Ernest Hemingway to the Irishman James Joyce, also thrived in this atmosphere of artistic freedom. In Paris, Cummings met another American poet, Ezra Pound, who had been living abroad since 1907. Pound was a leader in a literary movement called imagism, which flourished in the early twentieth century. Imagists strove for just the right words to create vivid pictures in readers' minds. One of Pound's most famous imagist poems, "In a Station of the Metro [Paris subway]," consists of two brief lines:

> The apparition of these faces in the crowd;
> Petals on a wet, black bough.

"Mr. Ezra Pound is a man of my own height,reddish goatee and ear whiskers,heavier built,moves nicely," Cummings observed. He said that Pound had a "gymnastic personality," that he was no ordinary person, but "somebody,and intricate." Cummings and Pound spent one long night walking the streets of Paris, with Pound, the better-known poet, advising Cummings about his work. Don't try to be "clever" all the time, Pound counseled. Although they would meet seldom, Cummings and Pound remained friends and exchanged letters for the rest of Cummings's life.

The Thayers had also come to Paris that spring—to get a divorce. In the 1920s, because of differences in French and American laws, it was easier to divorce in France than in the United States. Scofield Thayer had arrived in Paris with Slater Brown, whom he had hired as his private secretary.

Dos Passos boarded a train for the Middle East, but Estlin remained in Paris to be near Elaine and get to know Nancy, who was a year and a half old. After the divorce became final, on July 25, Scofield Thayer left for Vienna to be analyzed by Dr. Sigmund Freud. Freud had gained world-

Elizabeth Cummings as a young woman.

Artists of all kinds flocked to Paris in the 1920s. Among those pictured here are Ezra Pound (*middle row, right, wearing a large beret*), the American photographer Man Ray (*squatting, left, with a camera*), and the French writer Jean Cocteau (*squatting, right, with a cane*).

wide fame as the founder of psychoanalysis, a method of studying the unconscious mind. Many wealthy people journeyed to Austria to lie on Freud's couch and recall their early lives, hoping to gain self-knowledge. Brown moved in with Cummings, who spent much of his time with Elaine and Nancy. On most days, he met them at their stylish hotel and accompanied them to a park or café or puppet show. He called Nancy "Mopsy," and was charmed to hear her learn to speak.

That summer it seemed that everyone was in Paris. Edward Cummings had work to do in Europe for the World Peace Foundation, and in September, he visited his son, bringing important news: the firm of Boni and Liveright had agreed to publish Estlin's book. Estlin was thrilled, of course, but he and Slater Brown were about to leave on a bicycle tour of Italy, and he had no time to deal with publishers. He persuaded his father to oversee the project, but he did take time to inform the book's editor that his name was to appear in print as "E. E. Cummings (not E. Estlin, not Edward E., nor Edward Estlin)." He also selected the book's title: *The Enormous Room.*

Estlin and Slater crossed the Alps into northern Italy and bicycled as far south as Naples. They made frequent brief stops in cities and towns to see famous landmarks and sample the local wine. In November, they returned to Paris by train. Estlin decided to remain in the city he loved, to write and paint there, even though Elaine was ready to head home.

Rebecca Cummings, who met Elaine and Nancy in New York, took one look at the little girl and knew she was Estlin's child. She kept this knowledge to herself, though, at least for the time being, because Estlin had yet to accept Nancy as his own. He looked upon Nancy as Elaine's daughter, and Elaine as his girlfriend and nothing more. Yet he missed Elaine that winter. When she returned to Paris in May 1922 and he saw her walking toward him, he experienced his "life's most magical moment," he said. Once again, he spent joyful days with Elaine, and he doted on two-year-old Mopsy, laughing at her chatter, buying her balloons, and taking her on picnics. The days passed in ease and happiness.

Elaine had brought along four copies of *The Enormous Room,* which had been pub-

The view from his Paris window inspired Cummings to draw this picture.

lished in the United States, and Estlin held his finished book for the first time. His initial happiness rapidly turned to anger when he thumbed through the pages and saw that several chapters had been omitted, sentences he'd written in French had been translated into English, and misprints abounded. He wrote to his father to demand an explanation, and Edward Cummings replied that he took full responsibility. Boni and Liveright had made the changes, but he had let them stand rather than delay publication. He reminded Estlin that there might have been fewer mistakes if the author had come home to supervise the printing of his own book.

To the reading public, the cuts and mistakes hardly mattered. Whether they loved *The Enormous Room* or hated it, readers understood that this book was unlike any other. "Mr. Cummings has written a terrible book, but it is a profoundly beautiful book," commented one reviewer; "it is among the most beautiful that I have ever read."

"I feel as if I had been rooting long, desperate hours in a junk heap, irritably but thoroughly pawing over all sorts of queer, nameless garbage, rotting tin cans, owls' skeletons," wrote another, "and yet as if . . . I had come away at last with some lumps of curious, discolored but nonetheless precious metal."

Was *The Enormous Room* really terrible and beautiful, full of junk and precious metal at the same time?

Cummings had modeled his account on *The Pilgrim's Progress,* a seventeenth-century religious allegory by John Bunyan, a Puritan clergyman. In Bunyan's

Cummings's sketches of fellow prisoners at La Ferté-Macé. Some of these men are described in *The Enormous Room*.

novel, a Christian's journey from the City of Destruction to the Celestial City mirrors the soul's path from sin to salvation. The Christian wrestles with monsters and spiritual obstacles as he traverses the Valley of Humiliation and the Valley of the Shadow of Death. He must cross the River of Death before reaching his journey's end. Along the way, he meets characters named for their most notable traits, such as Mr. Worldly-Wise and Mr. Facing-Both-Ways.

In *The Enormous Room,* Cummings calls his own journey from ambulance service through imprisonment and release a pilgrimage. He gives names to his fellow prisoners that reflect their roles or characteristics. For example, he encounters John the Bathman, who escorts the prisoners to their baths, and the Bear, the man with lumbering movements. Even the foul-smelling bucket that serves as Cummings's toilet when he is locked up at Noyon briefly becomes a companion and gets a name: Ça Pue [That Stinks].

A pencil self-portrait from the 1920s. Throughout his adult life, Cummings created many drawings and paintings of himself.

The good-natured man of African descent is Jean le Nègre [Jean the Black]. Cummings recalls this prisoner with special fondness and in a section of poetic writing hopes to be remembered by him one day: "Take me up into your mind once or twice before I die(you know why:just because the eyes of you and me will be full of dirt some day). Quickly take me up into the bright child of your mind,before we both go suddenly all loose and silly."

Another favorite prisoner gets the name Zulu, because he is unlike anyone

Cummings has ever met, and to Cummings no one could be more foreign than a Zulu. This Zulu is not an African, but a Polish farmer who had been living in France with his family and has no idea why he is in prison. Cummings admires Zulu, who is at all times honest, immersed in the present, and one with his emotions. Cummings explains:

> Things which are always inside of us and in fact are us and which consequently will not be pushed off or away where we can begin thinking about them—are no longer things; they, and the us which they are equals A Verb; an IS.

He used the same word, "IS," when writing about the sculptor Gaston Lachaise. In the personal vocabulary of E. E. Cummings, artist and human being, the word *is* is very important. It means pure feeling, which is the highest state of awareness. Thought is a step below emotion, because by thinking we feel incompletely. Belief is lower still, a state of incomplete thought.

The Enormous Room was just the start of E. E. Cummings's career as a published author. In February 1922, when John Dos Passos stopped in Paris on his way back to the United States, Estlin pressed into his hands the manuscript for a book of poems titled *Tulips & Chimneys* and asked him to get it into print. Editors were willing to listen to Dos Passos, a novelist with a growing reputation, and in 1923, *Tulips and Chimneys* was on bookstore shelves in the United States. Estlin grumbled because the publisher, T. Seltzer, had trimmed the book from one hundred fifty-two poems to sixty-six and replaced the ampersand in the title with the word *and,* but he was pleased with the book overall.

Tulips and Chimneys summed up the poetry of the first part of Cumming's life. Included were "in Just- / spring," "Buffalo Bill's / defunct," "Epithalamion," "Puella Mea," and other poems familiar to Estlin's friends and readers of the *Dial.* The poet had divided the book into two parts, "Tulips," which contained the more experimental poems, and "Chimneys," which consisted of sonnets, a traditional poetic form, including "the Cambridge ladies who live in furnished souls."

In some of the "Tulips," Cummings tore words apart as a way of separating the sounds of syllables and letters from their meaning. He forced readers to proceed slowly, to relish these delicious sounds as they gradually put the words back together and discovered what the poem said:

i was considering how
within night's loose
sack a star's
nibbling in-

fin
-i-
tes-
i
-mal-
ly devours

darkness the
hungry star
which will e

-ven
tu-
al
-ly jiggle
the bait of
dawn and be jerked

into

eternity . . .

As a poet, Cummings continually asked himself, what else can language be made
to do?

The "Chimneys" dealt with love and unavoidable death. Some of the poems
described the beauty of the earth and the heavens:

notice the convulsed orange inch of moon
perching on this silver minute of evening . . .

Some were strikingly different from any sonnet that had been written before:

"kitty". sixteen,5'1",white,prostitute.

ducking always the touch of must and shall,
whose slippery body is Death's littlest pal,

skilled in quick softness. Unspontaneous. cute . . .

Reviewers loved the energy and playfulness in Cummings's poems. "He responds eagerly and unconstrainedly to all the world has to offer," one remarked. "The poet always seems to be having a glorious time with himself and his world," said another. Yet the same critics hated the oddities of Cummings's style. "His poems are hideous on the page," said the first. The second found Cummings's "eccentric system of typography" so irritating that when quoting his work in her review, she corrected his punctuation, capitalization, and spacing. The brazenness of this critic made Cummings furious!

Slater Brown and his wife, Susan Jenkins Brown, at their farm in Pawling, New York, during the winter of 1925–26.

Slater Brown connected the uniqueness of his friend's poetry to the fact that Cummings also was a painter, "because he has carried over the eye and method of art into the field of poetry. . . . To many of those who do not understand this fact," Brown observed, "the poems of E. E. Cummings seem nothing more than verbal mannerism."

Playful, eager Estlin was the perfect person to take Nancy to the circus in the spring of 1923. That summer, Elaine and Nancy vacationed in Biarritz, an elegant resort on the Bay of Biscay, and Estlin stayed in cheap lodgings nearby. Elaine, who was wealthy, traveled with servants and socialized with rich friends (people Estlin disliked), but he refused to let her support him. He made a show of being independent and needing to economize, although most of the money he lived on came from his father.

When Elaine and Nancy sailed for the United States in September 1923, Estlin stayed behind, nursing a sprained ankle. Alone in Paris, he took stock of himself. Scofield Thayer had examined his early life with Dr. Freud to gain insight into his present state of mind, so now Estlin delved into his own past. In his memory and on paper, he returned to the house on Irving Street and to Joy Farm, and he relived scenes that had been acted out there years earlier. He recalled his school days, childhood illnesses, and the books he had loved when he was small. He was trying to understand himself through this process, but he was also grappling with a big question: whether to marry Elaine.

Life was pushing him toward marriage. Not only were he and Elaine and Nancy starting to feel like a family, but he was establishing himself as a writer. His finances were improving, too. His father had given him a thousand dollars upon the publication of *Tulips and Chimneys,* and he had inherited another thousand dollars in October 1923, when Nana Cummings died. He was twenty-nine years old, but was he ready?

He still had not made up his mind about marriage later that fall when he received a letter from Elaine asking him to come home. He went anyway, and found a tiny apartment in Greenwich Village, near Elaine. He spent Christmas with Elaine and Mopsy and became more and more a part of their lives. Together, he and Nancy enjoyed outings to the zoo and to FAO Schwarz, New York's huge, wondrous toy store. He wrote fairy tales for private story hours.

At last, it was Elaine who proposed that they marry, and he said yes. The two talked about marriage and decided theirs had to be one in which both husband and wife felt happy and committed. They agreed on paper that if one partner ever wanted a divorce, the other would not object.

The wedding took place on March 19, 1924, at 104 Irving Street in Cambridge. The Reverend Cummings performed the ceremony, and Estlin's mother, sister, and aunt Jane attended. On April 25, Estlin adopted four-year-old Nancy, becoming her father in the eyes of the law. She kept the name Nancy Thayer, though, and she was never told about the adoption. At that time, adults commonly tried to protect children from information that might confuse or upset them and glossed over inconvenient truths in their own interactions.

(6)

G r i e f s   o f   J o y

I am nearest happiness," Estlin wrote that spring, believing he had com-
bined the best of married and single life. He had Elaine and Mopsy, but,
he said, "i do no work for them,i am free,i assume no responsibilities."
His daily routine changed very little after he moved in with his wife and child. He
came and went as he pleased, and thought nothing of going out with friends and
leaving Elaine alone. Painting and poetry still commanded most of his attention.

The marriage was only a few weeks old when Elaine's sister Constance, who
had been traveling, died unexpectedly of pneumonia in a New York City hotel.
Elaine was overcome with grief. She received a further shock when Estlin let
her make the funeral arrangements alone, without offering his help. If his wife
needed comfort or support, he failed to notice.

In May, Elaine left to spend the summer in Europe, taking Nancy. Estlin's days
were as happy-go-lucky when his family was away as when they were with him.
He slept late and breakfasted at Khoury's on baba gannouj. He saw friends in the
afternoon and at dinner, and worked long into the night. He submitted a painting,
Noise, Number Twelve, to the Independent Artists' Show of 1924, and he began a
portrait of Nancy.

Then, in June, he received an alarming letter from Elaine. She had written
from France to say that she wanted a divorce. While crossing the ocean, she had
fallen in love with another passenger aboard the ship, an Irish banker named
Frank MacDermot. Estlin was stunned. He told himself that she couldn't mean it,
that this was just a passing fancy. He was willing to believe any excuse.

When Elaine turned up without warning at the end of June, he finally understood that she was serious. "I know where I stand. And I know what I want," Elaine said. "And most difficult of all, I know when I have made a mistake."

Estlin begged her to stay with him. He had been happy; hadn't she been happy, too? Could she possibly wait a year? The pleading turned into shouting matches, with Elaine calling Estlin selfish and "like a child." She was determined to end the marriage as soon as possible.

Edward Cummings told his son to confront MacDermot and settle the matter with his fists, but Estlin lacked the will to fight. Deeply despondent, he bought a gun and composed suicide notes. On one frightening occasion, he stood before Elaine with the loaded pistol and threatened to blow his brains out while she looked on. As Elaine turned her back to him, Estlin remembered Mopsy and took control of himself. He removed the bullets from the gun, and there were no more dramatic threats.

How could this marriage ever work? Elaine failed to comprehend why Estlin refused to dress for dinner or be civil to her wealthy friends. And it seemed to him that she would never understand his devotion to art. At last, he decided to behave honorably, to "give her the divorce & live." As he explained to his mother, "I consider myself beaten by an unbeatable person whom I love & admire very much & whom I would like to have admire me since she cannot love me." He started writing a novel, *Edward Seul* [Edward Alone], based on the breakup of his marriage.

Elaine went to France to begin divorce proceedings, and Estlin moved into a room with good light for painting at 4 Patchin Place in Greenwich Village. Patchin Place was a quiet, gated courtyard, shaded by trees. Estlin's landlord was his old friend J. Sibley Watson.

French law required both husband and wife to live in France for a month before a divorce could be granted. By November 1, Estlin was in Paris, the scene of so much past happiness. He spent a day of play with Nancy, and he again urged Elaine to change her mind, if only for their child's sake.

But the divorce was granted on December 4, less than nine months after the wedding. Estlin felt so upset and helpless that he signed the divorce papers without securing the legal right to see Nancy. On the back of an envelope, he wrote the words he would say to his little playmate if he could:

Patchin Place in Greenwich Village, in a 1936 photograph. Cummings maintained a home here for most of his life.

Cummings's drawing of Nancy.

Goodbye dear & next time when I feel a little better we'll ride on the donkeys & next time on the pigs maybe or you will [ride] a bicycle & i will ride a swan & next time when my heart is all mended again with snow & repainted with bright new paint we'll ride you & I

He spent Christmas in Cambridge before returning to Patchin Place. Once his wounded emotions started to heal, he deeply regretted giving Elaine sole custody of their daughter. He sought help from his parents, and they turned to their attorney. Messages were cabled between the United States and France as the two sides bargained. At first, Elaine said she would allow Estlin to visit Nancy but would not give him legal custody for any part of the year. Estlin was ready to accept that offer, but the attorney persuaded Elaine to grant Estlin custody of Nancy for three months each year.

What happiness! Estlin looked forward to blissful summers with Mopsy at Joy Farm, and to teaching her to love one of the places he loved best in the world.

Edward and Rebecca Cummings still spent summers in the New Hampshire mountains. In 1925, Edward Cummings turned sixty-four, but he was as vigorous as ever. It came as a shock, therefore, when he was forced to retire. The South Congregational Church, where he had served for many years, joined with the First Church of Boston. The membership voted to retain the minister of the First Church, who was younger. The Reverend Cummings was given an honorary title, minister emeritus.

Now it was Estlin's turn to aid his father. He hurried to Cambridge, and as his father walked darkly toward him down the front steps of his home, Estlin told him why leaving the pulpit was a good thing. "In losing the church," Estlin said, "you've entered the world." Edward Cummings had such an expansive mind that "only a small part of you could possibly fit in that church," Estlin continued. "Now(for the first time in years)you're really you."

Edward Cummings put his shoulders back and stood a little taller. He said, "If you feel that way about me, I'll feel that way," and embraced his son.

The publication of two books of poetry in 1925 also brought Estlin happiness. One, *XLI Poems,* contained some new work, but most of the forty-one poems were leftovers from *Tulips and Chimneys.* These were poems from his college years describing twilight or the dawn or meditating on love. Cummings called them "harmless," because they were less experimental than his later pieces.

The other book was *&* [called *And*]. Cummings was determined to use the ampersand removed from the title of *Tulips and Chimneys.* He dedicated *&* to E. O., Elaine Orr. Many of the poems in this volume had been too daring for the editors of his other poetry books because they dealt with sex, prostitutes, or urban street life, with all its noise, color, and smells. For this reason, Cummings had arranged to publish this book privately, at his own expense. He was grateful that the printer he hired, Sam Jacobs, made sure the punctuation and capitalization were just as he wanted them.

As a poet, Cummings was still cutting diamonds as clear as the purest water, but their facets

Rebecca and Edward Cummings in the mid-1920s.

were irregular, and they reflected his unique conception of beauty. & contained challenging poems that kept readers' eyes and minds working. More than ever, Cummings had stretched out words and used punctuation marks and capital letters to add meaning or create visual and aural effects. By making language bright and new, he forced readers to take a fresh look at whatever he described.

Sometimes, he pried a word open with a phrase wrapped in parentheses to show that two events or thoughts occur at the same time:

> pigeons fly ingand
>
> whee(:are,SpRiN,kLiNg an in-stant with sunLight
> then)l-
> ing all go BlacK wh-eel-ing
>
> oh
>   ver
>   mYveRylitTle
>
> street
> where
> you will come,
>
>   at twi li ght
> s(oon & there's
> a   m oo
>)n.

Cummings used traditional four-line rhyming stanzas in a poem about the importance of thinking for oneself:

> here is little Effie's head
> whose brains are made of gingerbread
> when the judgment day comes
> God will find six crumbs . . .

The crumbs tell God their names: "may," "might," "should," "could," "would," and "must." They exist because Effie has always done as she was told and never dared to question, because she is "Effie who isn't alive."

In 1925, Cummings received the Dial Award for his contribution to literature. Scofield Thayer had established this award, which came with two thousand dollars, to honor outstanding contributors to his magazine. He gave eight Dial Awards between 1921 and 1928, to such important writers as Ezra Pound, T. S. Eliot, and Marianne Moore. Cummings was grateful for the money and for the recognition. The prize boosted his reputation and persuaded his publisher Horace Liveright to ask for another book of poems and reissue *The Enormous Room* with all the errors and omissions corrected.

The poet Hart Crane, Cummings's friend.

That year, new friends had entered Cummings's life. One was Hart Crane, a twenty-six-year-old poet from Ohio who lived hard and drank heavily. A federal law known as the Volstead Act had outlawed the sale of most alcoholic beverages in the United States beginning in 1920, so during their long nights on the town, Cummings and Crane went from one speakeasy, or illegal bar, to another. At the time, Crane was writing his masterwork, *The Bridge,* a long poem that employed the Brooklyn Bridge as its central image.

The friendship thrived, although the two men saw different things in each other. Cummings claimed that "Crane's mind was no bigger than a pin, but it didn't matter; he was a born poet." Crane confided to a friend that Cummings was one of his favorite people to talk to in New York. He called *The Enormous Room* "a permanently beautiful thing," but he thought Cummings's poetry lacked discipline. If he "only cared to take a little more pains and organize—he'd be superb," Crane said.

Estlin also met Anne Barton, a pert, pretty woman who had a young daughter and was recently divorced. Anne had been an artist's model, and she enjoyed posing for him. She loved parties and good times, and she made him laugh. Friends

Anne Barton,
photographed in 1927.

said that to be with Estlin and Anne was loads of fun. "If I had my way would take both [Cummings] and Anne along with me to heaven when I go," Hart Crane wrote.

Jolly companions helped to ease Estlin's disappointment when he learned he would be spending the summer without his Mopsy. Elaine and Frank MacDermot had married and settled in Tuxedo Park, a town near New York City. MacDermot opposed Nancy's visiting her father, mostly because he worried about his family's reputation. What would their wealthy neighbors think if an artist without much money showed up and claimed to be Nancy's father? Was it not better for Frank, Elaine, and Nancy to put the past behind them?

MacDermot turned up at 4 Patchin Place to deliver a threat. "Even if Elaine, by some freak of fate, consented to being separated from the child this summer, I should fight it tooth and nail," he said. If Estlin insisted on his rights, then MacDermot would whisk Elaine and Nancy away to live in Ireland.

A friend put Estlin in touch with a different lawyer. This time, the news was discouraging. The custody agreement, which had been drafted by Elaine's attorney, was flawed, the lawyer said. What was more, courts almost always decided in favor of the mother in custody cases. Elaine was more financially secure than Estlin, and able to provide a stable home in a traditional family setting. Estlin understood that he "would have not one chance in a million" of winning a case in court.

The MacDermots did permit Cummings to have three brief visits with Nancy, accompanied by her nanny, in late 1925 or early 1926. It is thought that these visits took place in public settings, such as Central Park in New York City. Cummings explored the feelings of a divorced father in the unfinished *Edward Scul* manuscript. When the fictional Edward watched his six-year-old daughter hop on one foot or jump rope, he felt stirrings along "the inner fringes of his heart."

Stirrings of the heart, whether from pain or from gladness, inspired Cummings to write poems. He was "obsessed by Making." As he explained in the foreword to his next book of poetry, "If a poet is anybody,he is somebody to whom things made matter very little." In other words, finished work was over and done, and held no interest for him. It was the new poems—those in the making—that got him excited. The makers of the world were open to all possibilities, even the most unexpected. "Whereas nonmakers must content themselves with the merely undeniable fact that two times two is four," Cummings wrote, the poet "rejoices in a purely irresistible truth(to be found,in abbreviated costume,upon the title page of the present volume)." The volume was titled *is 5*.

One of the most talked-about works in this lively book, "Poem, or Beauty Hurts Mr. Vinal," is filled with brand names, advertising slogans, fragments of patriotic songs, and slang, which Cummings called "the most alive aspect of a language":

>   take it from me kiddo
>   believe me
>   my country, 'tis of
>
>   you,land of the Cluett
>   Shirt Boston Garter and Spearmint
>   Girl With The Wrigley Eyes(of you
>   land of the Arrow Ide
>   and Earl &
>   Wilson
>   Collars)of you i
>   sing . . .

Radio had recently begun bringing entertainment into people's homes, and Cummings hated the catchy ads that had become the poetry of modern life. (There would be no radio at 4 Patchin Place.) Many readers guessed that the Mr. Vinal in the poem's title was Harold Vinal, secretary of the Poetry Society of America, who opposed modern trends in poetry. Using Vinal's name also allowed Cummings to broaden the meaning of his poem. The synthetic material vinyl was developed in the early 1920s, so Mr. Vinal may also represent the plastic person whose life is defined by ads and clichés.

Cummings took aim as well at science. By calculating the size and scope of natural phenomena, scientists destroyed people's wonder at the beauty all around them—or so the poet believed. He wrote:

> (While you and i have lips and voices which
> are for kissing and to sing with
> who cares if some oneeyed son of a bitch
> invents an instrument to measure Spring with?

Science was a product of thought, the mental process one step removed from feeling. The thinkers of the world held themselves back from complete experience, Cummings insisted:

> since feeling is first
> who pays any attention
> to the syntax of things
> will never wholly kiss you . . .

In a brief, beautiful poem he reminded readers that life is short, death is final, and love is precious:

> in spite of everything
> which breathes and moves,since Doom
> (with white longest hands
> neatening each crease)
> will smooth entirely our minds
>
> —before leaving my room
> i turn,and(stooping
> through the morning)kiss
> this pillow,dear
> where our heads lived and were.

In 1927, the composer Aaron Copland set this poem to music in a short piece titled "Poet's Song."

In March 1926, Cummings went to Europe with Anne Barton and her four-year-old daughter, Diana. He showed them his favorite sights in Paris: sidewalk cafés, the circus, and the Louvre. Estlin and Anne saw the African-American dancer and singer Josephine Baker perform at the Folies Bergere, the famous

Parisian music hall. During World War I, African-American fighting men had introduced Europeans to jazz. Now, the French were crazy for jazz and African-American performers. Baker was a highly paid star in Paris. She danced and sang wearing next to nothing, and Cummings remarked that she had "an entirely beautiful body and a beautiful command of its entirety."

Italy, this time, was less to his liking. Premier Benito Mussolini had transformed the government into a single-party, totalitarian dictatorship. He controlled squads of black-shirted Fascists who beat up communists, socialists, liberals, and anyone else who disagreed openly with official policy. The "singularly uncheerful" face of Mussolini stared at Estlin, Anne, and Diana from posters glued to houses, railroad stations, and fences, as "Black Shirts" arrogantly shouldered tourists off sidewalks.

Josephine Baker

Phot. v. Gudenberg

The American-born performer Josephine Baker as featured on a cigarette trading card. At one time, cigarettes came with collectible cards depicting anything from celebrities to military ships and planes to flowers and butterflies.

Estlin wondered where Mussolini would set his sights next. He imagined Italian troops marching across the border to take control of France.

In July 1926, Anne and Diana resumed their life in New York, and Estlin went to Silver Lake—again without Nancy. He intended to write a play, like John Dos Passos and other authors who were writing experimental works for the theater. Dos Passos's play *The Garbage Man* had been performed in Greenwich Village in March 1926. It was an attempt "to fuse the two halves of the New York theatre: the 'serious' half that strives for content and that at present attains mostly a lot of empty seats, and the boxoffice half that has, for musical shows, farces and melodramas at least, the technique of showmanship," Dos Passos said. *The Garbage Man* tackled such serious themes as conformity, intolerance, and consumerism, but it also featured a noisy parade.

Estlin returned to New York in the fall with his play nearly complete. On the evening of November 2, 1926, he and Anne were relaxing at the home of

Premier Benito Mussolini, surrounded by his staff, peers over
his shoulder during a Fascist celebration in Rome in 1923.

M. R. Werner, a fellow writer, when his sister arrived unexpectedly. Her face ashen,
Elizabeth asked to speak to Estlin alone. Werner ushered them to a private room,
where Elizabeth said there had been a terrible accident. Their parents had run into a
snowstorm while driving through the Ossipee Mountains of New Hampshire, on
their way to Silver Lake. Barely able to see where they were headed, they drove onto
railroad tracks, and their car was split in two by a fast-moving train. Their father was
dead, killed instantly, and their mother lay in a country hospital, on the verge of death.

Estlin and Elizabeth wasted no time and caught the next train to New
Hampshire. As they stood at their mother's bedside, the doctor caring for Rebecca
Cummings explained that she had been found standing at the accident scene with
blood pouring from her fractured skull. Only when she saw that her husband's
body was properly covered would she let anyone attend to her. Her hideous wound
had finally been stitched by candlelight, because the snowstorm had caused a
power failure. The doctor wondered how she could be alive.

He knew nothing of his patient's determination, though. Hearing the voices of her children, Rebecca decided she would not let them lose her. She forced herself to rally, and within days, she was well enough to be transferred by ambulance to a Boston hospital. Yet all the time, she insisted there was still something wrong with her head. When surgeons in Boston brought her into the operating room and reopened her incision, Rebecca remained awake and watched the procedure with a hand mirror. Later, she showed off a small bottle containing the dirt and splinters the surgeons had removed from her head. "You see?" she exclaimed. "I was right!"

One parent had survived, but one was lost. Estlin memorialized his father in a long poem that explored the contradictions in Edward Cummings's personality. In this poem, he also recalled his father's optimism and honesty, and presented him as the towering figure he had been to his son:

> my father moved through dooms of love
> through sames of am through haves of give,
> singing each morning out of each night
> my father moved through depths of height . . .
>
> Lifting the valleys of the sea
> my father moved through griefs of joy;
> praising a forehead called the moon
> singing desire into begin . . .
>
> because my father lived his soul
> love is the whole and more than all

(7)

T h e   H i g h   W i r e

*I*t looks like something from an amusement park: a flat surface on which someone has painted a doctor and his female patient. Holes have been cut where their faces belong, and through these jut the heads of a living man and woman. Before them sit three old women who are rocking, knitting, and talking nonsense like the weird sisters in the opening scene of *Macbeth.* "We call our hippopotamus It's Toasted." "I wish my husband didn't object to them." "Of course it's a bother to clean the cage every day."

So begins E. E. Cummings's play *Him.*

Him is about a woman named Me and the man in her life, called Him. Each is involved in a creative struggle. As Me prepares to give birth, Him tries to write a play. In act one, action shifts between the hospital room of the opening scene and the apartment of Him and Me, where the two appear to be carrying on different conversations. Me tries to probe their relationship, but Him wants to talk about his writing.

Him says, "Imagine a human being who balances three chairs, one on top of another, on a wire, eighty feet in the air with no net underneath, and then climbs into the top chair, and begins to swing. . . ." This was how Cummings felt whenever he wrote a poem or painted a picture. Artists were circus acrobats who attempted impossible feats high in the air. Creating meant taking chances, and to Cummings the high wire was the best possible place to be. As Him explains, "I am this trick, I sway—selfish and smiling and careful—above all the people."

In act two, Him shows Me parts of his unfinished play, which are presented as short, sometimes humorous sketches. An Englishman lugs a heavy trunk that represents his unconscious mind; two businessmen exchange identities when each wears a mask that resembles the other. One skit shows Mussolini dressed as Napoleon and acting like a buffoon. Then, in act three, a circus freak show leads up to the birth of Me's child.

Him was an unusual play, but the managers of the Provincetown Playhouse were looking for something different. They wanted to attract theatergoers to Greenwich Village with plays that were unlike anything that could be seen elsewhere. They decided to present *Him* as soon as they read it, even though it was a tough play to produce. Not only were there twenty-one scene changes, but the scenery was complex. Him and Me's apartment was to have four walls, three solid and one invisible. Each time the apartment was shown, the room turned clockwise, and a different wall became invisible. Casting was another challenge, because Cummings's play called for seventy-two characters and extra players for crowd scenes. At the Provincetown Playhouse, to save money, thirty actors played all the roles. As a result, one actor had to change costumes eighteen times in the first act. Another wore four costumes, one over another, in order to switch roles quickly.

All through the early weeks of 1928, when *Him* was in rehearsal, Cummings could be found at the Provincetown Playhouse. He even ate lunch with the actors at the speakeasy across the street. Cummings "was around all the time, but he didn't interfere with the rehearsals," said the play's director, James Light. "When the actors wanted a reading of a line, they went to Cummings. They found out more from him than I ever could give them in direction."

Light added, "His greatest characteristic, of course, was his cheerfulness."

Him opened on a Wednesday night, April 18, 1928, to a sold-out theater. As the audience glanced at their programs and waited for the show to begin, they read a baffling "warning" from the playwright, whose name was printed in lowercase letters. "*him* isn't a comedy or a tragedy or a farce or a melodrama or a revue or an operetta or a moving picture or any other convenient excuse for going to the theatre—in fact, it's a PLAY, so let it PLAY," Cummings had written. "DON'T TRY TO UNDERSTAND IT, LET IT TRY TO UNDERSTAND YOU."

(Then as now, because Cummings followed his own rules of capitalization, many people wrongly thought that he never capitalized anything, including his name. It has become so common to see "e. e. cummings" in books that readers often think this is what the author favored. When it came to his name, however, Cummings followed tradition and preferred E. E. Cummings.)

A scene from *Him,* drawn by the artist John Sloan in 1928. In this scene from act two, African-American singers perform "Frankie and Johnny," a traditional song about love gone wrong.

The next day, when Cummings, Light, and the cast read the reviews, they saw that nearly all the critics hated the play. The critics seemed to be having a contest to see who could think up the worst adjectives to describe it. One said *Him* was "fatiguing, pretentious and empty." Another called it "incoherent, illiterate, preposterous balderdash, as completely and unremittingly idiotic as the human mind, when partly sober, can imagine."

Some reviewers devoted more energy to commenting on Cummings's warning than to saying anything worthwhile about the play. Responding to the playwright's advice to let *Him* "understand you," one said that he "projected himself across the footlights, hoping to be understood. It was no use."

Audiences, however, loved *Him*. The play might not have made sense, but it was fun to watch and even more fun to talk about. People came back to see it three and four times. "Now, if Mr. Cummings will only write a 'Her,'" said one fan. But soon the excitement was over. The complex scenery and large cast made *Him* a costly play to produce. Even with a full house every night, the small Provincetown Playhouse was losing money. *Him* closed after twenty-seven performances.

"I am very proud of doing this play," James Light said of *Him*. "We gave the bird a chance to sing." *Him* had drawn a young, sophisticated crowd to the Provincetown Playhouse, so despite their losses, the managers announced that they planned to produce another play by E. E. Cummings in 1929.

In truth, Cummings's play was years ahead of its time. It laid groundwork for theater of the absurd, a movement that emerged in Paris after World War II. Beginning in the late 1940s, Samuel Beckett, Eugène Ionesco, and other absurdist playwrights wrote dramas with seeming nonsense dialogue and illogical plots. Their purpose was to comment on the peculiar nature of human existence.

One person who liked *Him* was William Carlos Williams, who was a friend of Ezra Pound. Williams was both a poet and a physician in Rutherford, New Jersey. After seeing the play, Williams invited Cummings to dinner on a Sunday at one o'clock. One o'clock came and went, so Williams ventured out to find his guest. "I shall not forget the impression I got of a lone person meandering up a deserted Park Avenue stopping at every store window to look intently in at the shoes, ladies' wear, now and then a bank window perhaps, or at an Easter card, or at a brace and bit in Dow's hardware store," Williams recalled.

Williams's mother was keeping house for her son while his wife visited their boys at school in Europe. She served a chicken dinner and questioned Cummings about his family. The Williamses had a litter of Persian kittens, and the three adults played with them after dinner on the dining-room table. The kittens reminded Cummings of "birds in the nest," Williams said. "It was a nice afternoon. Mother thought him gentle but strange."

When *Him* was published as a book, it contained this dedication:

> looking forward into the past or looking
> backward into the future I
> walk on the highest
> hills and
> I laugh
> about
> it
> all
> the way
> ANNE BARTON

Estlin continued to see Anne, but their relationship was a troubled one. Again and again, they argued, broke up, and then reconciled. Only at Joy Farm were they always happy. In the fall of 1928, Estlin began psychoanalysis with Dr. Fritz Wittels, who had trained with Freud in Vienna. Over the next few months, with Wittels's help, he learned to understand himself a little better. At thirty-four, he vowed to grow up and assume the responsibilities of adult life.

Part of being responsible was marrying Anne, which he did on May 1, 1929, at a church in New York City. John Dos Passos was best man, and Estlin's sister and mother attended. Rebecca Cummings now lived in New York City to be near her children.

Over the next two years, Estlin and Anne made several trips to Europe, but they spent the summers with Diana in New Hampshire. Rebecca Cummings had given them Joy Farm, and Anne loved the old farmhouse. She had it painted white and bought new furniture for the downstairs rooms. She acquired a hen and chicks and two dogs. Estlin built a playhouse for Diana and a study in the woods for himself, and the music of saws and hammers accompanied daily life, as it had when Edward Cummings was alive. Estlin also installed a generator so the family could enjoy electric light at night.

The Cummingses entertained many guests at Joy Farm, but one person was plainly absent: Nancy. Elaine wanted Estlin to have no role in his daughter's life. If Estlin or his mother sent Nancy gifts, it was Elaine who thanked them. This made them suspect that Nancy never saw their presents. In February 1927, Elaine asked Estlin to cancel the adoption, but he angrily refused. Rebecca Cummings, who was just as angry as her son, sent Elaine a curt letter. "I have been, and still am, ready and eager to have N [Nancy] at any time and to pay her expenses while she is with me—You have always refused to let her come, even for a visit, and E [Estlin] has been repeatedly denied, even his right to see her," Rebecca wrote. "You will pardon me if I cannot see that to be E's daughter will be injurious to N."

Elaine relented and invited Estlin to see his child on March 4. He and seven-year-old Nancy were never alone during this visit—Elaine and Frank MacDermot and Estlin's old friend Stewart Mitchell were present as well. Later, Estlin reported to his mother, "She looked pale,and Elaine said she was underweight and small for her age—you may imagine my reaction—but Nancy and I had a wonderful time walking up and down the room,joking,imitating each other,and making fun of things in general." Estlin and Nancy drew pictures for each other, and he displayed hers on the mantelpiece at Patchin Place.

A month later, the MacDermots moved to Ireland, taking Nancy out of Estlin's life. She would grow up believing that Scofield Thayer was her father.

Among the guests at Joy Farm were John Dos Passos and his new wife, Katy. Dos Passos had just completed *Nineteen Nineteen,* a novel about the United States during World War I that was set against the backdrop of world events. A major event of those years had been the Russian Revolution. Political upheaval had begun in Russia in March 1917, with the overthrow of the monarchy. In November, the Bolshevik Party, a workers' party led by Vladimir Lenin, mounted an armed rebellion and ousted the provisional government. In the new state that was established, the Union of Soviet Socialist Republics (USSR, or Soviet Union), Lenin's government abolished the right to private property. The government owned all the factories and farms, and each person worked for the good of all.

The USSR was a great political and social experiment. Many young, educated Americans hoped the Soviet system would lead to equality for all citizens and a fair distribution of wealth, and they paid close attention to events in the new nation. Dos Passos had visited the Soviet Union in 1928 and returned full of optimism.

Cummings still believed in finding things out for himself—just as he did in 1922, when he counseled his sister—even if it meant taking his own trip to the USSR. In January 1931, while he and Anne and Diana were staying in France, he began studying Russian with a Ukrainian woman who had fled from the city of Odessa during the 1917 revolution. By early May, he knew enough Russian to get by and was ready to go.

In the 1930s, only a few thousand foreign tourists traveled to the USSR each year. Many more went to France, Italy, and other European countries. The official Soviet travel agency, Intourist, welcomed foreign visitors, because tourism gave the government a chance to spread propaganda. Intourist arranged for foreigners to see museums, factories, and other sites and to meet Soviet citizens engaged in their own lines of work. Farmers met farmers, teachers met teachers, and writers met writers. However, many westerners in the USSR felt conscious of being under Intourist's ever-watchful eye.

The long train trip from Paris to Moscow took Cummings through Germany and Poland. He reached the Soviet capital expecting to be met by Vladimir Lidin, a playwright, but his guide was nowhere in sight. With no place to stay and not sure what to do, he turned to Intourist. He was assigned a room at the Metropole, one of Moscow's few luxury hotels, which was well beyond his budget. He felt less alone

Henry Wadsworth Longfellow Dana stands on the porch of his grandfather's Cambridge house wearing the costume of a Russian Cossack. The contents of the packages piled next to him are a mystery. He collected Longfellow's papers and manuscripts, but he took meticulous care of these, so scholars think the packages must have contained something else.

when he discovered that Henry Wadsworth Longfellow Dana of Cambridge, grandson of the poet Henry Wadsworth Longfellow, was staying at the Metropole as well.

Professor Dana had come to the USSR to study Soviet theater. He took Estlin to see plays and introduced him to Soviet and American residents of Moscow, but he had no luck finding his new friend cheaper lodging. He put Estlin in touch with an American couple who were moving out of a new housing complex, but their flat was infested with bedbugs and next to a filthy toilet that all the tenants shared. Estlin turned it down. In his second week of searching, he met some friendly Americans, Charles and Joan Malamuth, who offered him a couch in their study. Charles Malamuth was an expert in Slavic languages who was reporting on Soviet life for a U.S. newspaper.

Cummings did some sightseeing. In Moscow's Red Square, he joined the crowd filing through Lenin's tomb. The preserved body of the first Soviet leader had been on display since 1924, the year he died. Cummings also saw the inside of a model prison on a tour conducted by Intourist, and he sat through a disappointing circus: "2 clowns,sad, costumeless,almost makeupless," he noted.

Overall, the USSR was as drab and depressing as that circus. Cummings called it "a world of Was—everything shoddy;everywhere dirt and cracked fingernails." He could easily tolerate the filth, bad food, and lack of toilet paper. After all, he had spent months as a prisoner. Instead, it was the absence of laughter and joy that made Soviet life so grim. And then there was the constant surveillance. One evening, Cummings and Dana discussed the Soviet system while sitting in a Moscow nightclub. As their talk grew more and more heated, the two Americans became aware of men from the GPU—the government police force—moving closer and closer. They wisely toned down their conversation.

The GPU was an instrument of terror that gave Soviet leader Joseph Stalin the power of a dictator. GPU agents imprisoned, tortured, and executed alleged spies, traitors, and enemies of the state. Anyone who openly criticized the government was subject to arrest and might never be seen again. Cummings encountered the GPU twice more while traveling by train to Kiev and Odessa. The uniformed officers searched every passenger compartment and demanded to see passports.

Mail delivery was another ordeal. Cummings received no letters during the first two weeks of his stay and just one after three weeks of waiting. Either censors were seizing his mail, or the Soviet postal system was letting it go astray. He was eager to hear from Anne, but when he finally did, the news was bad. Anne's first husband had committed suicide, so she was proceeding to the United States to tend to financial matters.

Anne was on Estlin's mind in Odessa, where the weight of Soviet oppression was lighter than in Moscow. For the first time since coming to the Soviet Union, Estlin saw lovers walking hand in hand and heard carefree laughter. On the shores of the Black Sea, he saw vacationers having mud baths, which they believed offered health benefits. People lay on the beach coated in black ooze and wearing little clothing. It was impossible to tell if one stocky man wore swimming trunks or just a thick layer of mud!

After six days in Odessa, Estlin boarded a steamship bound for Istanbul, where he would begin the long journey to Joy Farm. As the ship headed toward freedom, he filled his lungs with sea air, relaxed, and reflected on the experience of the past five weeks. He recoiled so strongly from the commercial side of American life that he had expected to like the Soviet Union. Instead, he was sickened by the way the Soviets repressed creativity and openness, two qualities he valued. "Russia, I felt, was more deadly than war," he said. He went on to explain that when nations do battle, "they hate by merely killing and maiming human beings." But the Soviets "hate by categorying and pigeonholing human beings." There was no room in the USSR for the human spirit.

After having seen tyranny firsthand, Estlin Cummings championed personal freedom more than ever before. His beliefs became hardened, and some people found him intolerant of different viewpoints. His friends quickly learned not to discuss socialism in his presence.

Noise, Number 13, a painting by F. E. Cummings. He described this painting in a poem that was included in *ViVa:*

> Concentric geometries of transparency slightly
> joggled sink through algebras of proud
> inwardlyness to collide spirally with iron
> arithmetics . . .
> uPDownwardishly
> find everywheres noisecoloured
> curvecorners gush silently perpetuating
> solids(More
> fluid than gas

Yet he remained light-hearted and spontaneous in his work and published three books in 1930 and 1931. One was a book with no title that was a compilation of nonsense stories and line drawings. Another, *CIOPW,* was a collection of his art. The letters in the title stand for the materials he used: charcoal, ink, oil, pencil, and watercolor. In this book were playful pictures of circus acrobats, dancers, and elephants. Two had been drawn on the backs of canceled checks, and one was on a page torn from a sketchbook. Cummings now painted recognizable subjects: human figures, landscapes, flowers, and portraits of loved ones, friends, and himself.

The third new work, *W,* was a book of poems. Cummings had often seen the letter W painted on walls in Europe by anonymous hands. It represented two *V*s side by side, a symbol for *viva* or *vive,* which mean "live" in the romance languages. In fact, this collection of seventy poems is usually referred to as *ViVa.* In *ViVa,* Cummings performed some of his most daring acrobatics. For example, in poem XXXVIII he captured the flash, clap, and rumble of a thunderstorm:

n(o)w

       the

how

  dis(appeared cleverly)world

iS Slapped:with;lightning

!

  at

which(shal)lpounceupcrackw(ill)jumps

of

  THuNdeRB

    loSSo!M . . .

Poem XLIII, in contrast, is a loving tribute to his mother that begins:

if there are any heavens my mother will(all by herself)have
one. It will not be a pansy heaven nor
a fragile heaven of lilies-of-the-valley but
it will be a heaven of blackred roses . . .

Cummings imagines his father in this heaven, too. And he leaves some words unwritten, reminding us of the way speech can trail off into thought, and how words unspoken can still be understood:

> my father will be(deep like a rose
> tall like a rose)
>
> standing near my
>
> swaying over her . . .

The voice fades away again in a whispered endearment: "This is my beloved my. . . ."

In *ViVa,* Cummings finally memorialized the soldier from Camp Devens who was imprisoned for refusing to fight. He had forgotten the man's name, so he called him Olaf:

> i sing of Olaf glad and big
> whose warmest heart recoiled at war:
> a conscientious object-or . . .

The traditional meter and rhyme scheme of this poem make its brutal imagery of torture all the more disturbing:

> "but—though all kinds of officers
> (a yearning nation's blueeyed pride)
> their passive prey did kick and curse . . .
> and egged the firstclassprivates on
> his rectum wickedly to tease
> by means of skillfully applied
> bayonets roasted hot with heat—
> Olaf(upon what once were knees)
> does almost ceaselessly repeat
> "there is some shit I will not eat" . . .

Desperate men hope to make a few pennies at a junk market on Houston Street, New York City, in 1933.

The poet asks his readers to remember Olaf, who was a finer person than most of us: "more brave than me:more blond than you."

Cummings had never earned much from his writing, but sales of these books were especially modest, mostly because people simply had no money to buy them. In 1931, the United States was in the second year of the Great Depression, the worst economic crisis in its history. Following the stock market crash of October 1929, thousands of banks and businesses folded. Millions of people had lost their jobs and their savings. The Provincetown Playhouse had closed its doors, and the *Dial* had shut down its presses.

With eight million workers unemployed, America struggled to cope. Breadlines wound around blocks in New York and elsewhere as churches and charities fed many of the hungry. Piles of furniture on city sidewalks represented families who had been evicted from their homes. In 1931, two hundred thousand families nationwide lost their houses or farms because they failed to make mortgage payments. There was no federal program for aiding the needy, and states and private organizations ran through their relief funds.

Estlin and Anne were staying afloat financially, thanks to the monthly allowance of a hundred dollars they received from Rebecca Cummings, but their marriage was rapidly sinking. Anne had started drinking heavily, and alcohol poisoned her tongue. She made cruel fun of Rebecca and Elizabeth, and she belittled Estlin in front of his friends, calling him "my puny husband." When a shocked listener asked why she stayed with Estlin if she detested him so, Anne shot back, "I want that property." She was determined to keep Joy Farm. Estlin bore the humiliation, because a divorce might mean losing the mountain home he loved. By June 1932, though, the matter was out of his hands, because Anne had met another man. She went to Mexico to get a divorce and came back to the United States to claim her share of Joy Farm.

For a second time Cummings waged a legal battle to protect what he believed was rightly his. On advice from a lawyer, he told Anne he would dispute the validity of the Mexican divorce in court. Anne begged him not to do that. She promised to give up her claim to Joy Farm—but she wanted the furniture she had bought for the farmhouse and thirty-five hundred dollars from Rebecca Cummings. Estlin was ready to agree to her offer, but his lawyer advised him to wait and force Anne to accept his terms. As Estlin explained to his mother, "Yes, she can have whatever furniture she put into the farm;No,she can't have 1(one)cent,let alone any dollars." Most importantly, she had to deed her share of Joy Farm to Rebecca. "Everybody is to lie low,*put nothing in writing where Anne is concerned,*" Estlin instructed his mother.

The strategy worked. Anne remarried in October 1932 and signed over her share of Joy Farm to her former mother-in-law. In return, Estlin agreed not to contest the divorce. This time, he had won.

(8)

N e v e r   B o r n   E n o u g h

*T*hrough all the turmoil, strange, gentle Estlin Cummings kept writing. He filled page after page until he had completed a long book about his trip to the Soviet Union. He took its title, *Eimi*, from the Greek word for "I am": "'A' as in a, 'me' as in me; accent on the 'me'": a-*me*. The perplexing title was a clue that Cummings was performing a literary high-wire act.

Eimi was full of linguistic experiments. Cummings sprinkled Russian words throughout the text. He created his own words, using negative prefixes and suffixes to stress what was missing in the society he visited. Soviet women, who lacked the stylish, feminine attire of Western Europe, became "nonmen"; an "unbanklike bank" was one that was filthy, inefficient, and all but useless.

Cummings tried to make the journey through the Soviet Union feel real and immediate to readers. Using a technique called stream of consciousness, he presented thoughts, feelings, and impressions just as they passed through his mind, one right after another. Some of the book was as abstract as Gertrude Stein's "little sales ladies."

Here is how Cummings described waiting in line to file through Lenin's tomb:

facefacefaceface
  hand-
      fin-
         claw

foot-

    hoof

(tovarich)

        es to number of numberlessness(un

-smiling)

with dirt's dirt dirty dirtier with others' dirt with dirt of themselves dirtiest waitstand
dirtily never smile shufflebudge dirty pausehalt

Smilingless.

       Some from nowhere (faces of nothing) others out of somewhere (something-
shaped hands) these knew ignorance (hugest feet and believing) those were friendless
(stooping in their deathskins) all—

numberlessly

—eachotherish

facefacefaceface

facefaceface

faceface

Face

   : all(of whom-which move-do-not-move numberlessly)Toward

the

  Tomb

     Crypt

        Shrine

A decade earlier, Cummings had modeled *The Enormous Room* on John Bunyan's
The Pilgrim's Progress. In *Eimi,* he refers to another famous allegory, *The Inferno,* written by Dante Alighieri in the fourteenth century. Dante imagined a journey through
Hell with the Roman poet Virgil as his guide. In *Eimi,* Cummings often uses the
name Virgil for Professor Dana, to let readers know that in this book the USSR is
Hell on Earth. But Cummings was a complex performer, and sometimes Dana is
called Sybil, the name of a witch or female prophet in Greek mythology.

Cummings changes identity in the book, too. At times, he is Comrade "Kem-
min-kz," which is how Russian speakers pronounced his last name, or simply
Comrade K. At other times, he is Cummings the American, Peesahtel and
Hoodozhnik (writer and painter), or I or me. Occasionally, several of these identities are present at once. Cummings wanted to show how fragmented he felt, how

Soviet oppression made it nearly impossible to be fully himself. But he certainly kept readers on their toes!

Getting *Eimi* into print presented obstacles. The linotype machines on which the book was being typeset kept breaking down. Cummings suspected that the operators had communist leanings and objected to the anti-Soviet tone of the book, and that they were deliberately holding up the project. He knew this was true when one typesetter spoke out against something he had written. He persuaded the book's publisher, the firm of Covici-Friede, to hire Sam Jacobs, the man who had printed *&*, to set the type by hand.

In March 1933, Jacobs printed 1,381 copies of *Eimi*—a very small number—because Covici-Friede had orders for just that many. The author signed each one. There was a second printing a year later, and these books were unsigned. *Eimi* sold poorly, though, not only because the Depression prevented people from spending money, but also because the book was very hard to read. One reviewer dubbed it "The Worst Book of the Month." When a new edition was issued in 1958, Cummings wrote a preface in which he explained *Eimi*'s title, subject, structure, and characters, and defined the Russian words in the text. Even with this help,

Marion Morehouse, photographed in the early 1930s.

though, very few people have read *Eimi* from beginning to end.

But some readers finished *Eimi* and liked it very much. The poet Marianne Moore considered it "a large poem." From Italy, Ezra Pound playfully wrote, "Oh well Whell hell itza great woik." But he also gave Cummings some professional advice: "The longer a work is, the more and longer [should] be the passages that are perfectly clear and simple to read."

Writers learn valuable lessons from every book they write, and move on. Cummings, who strived to be fully alive—to be an "IS"—approached life with hope. On the evening of June 23, 1932, he attended a play with the director James Light and his wife and met a woman who had a small part in the show. Beautiful Marion Morehouse was an actor and fashion model, and Cummings took her to dinner.

At first, Estlin thought he and this young woman were wrong for each other. He was thirty-seven, twelve years older than Marion. And she was three or four inches taller than he was. Yet these differences seemed not to bother Marion, and soon Estlin ignored them, too. He and Marion got along well. Although he was going through his second divorce, he started seeing her regularly. They walked to the aquarium where he had sketched sea lions, and they stood and watched the tugboats in New York Harbor. They often stopped in to see Rebecca Cummings, and the two women formed a warm friendship. Estlin could not know it then, but he had found the woman with whom he would spend the rest of his life.

Estlin had no telephone, so the couple communicated through letters and telegrams. "You're such a wonderfully marvelous Comrade, Kemminkz, and I'm so much in love with you I don't know what to do," Marion wrote. "I might fly the Atlantic up and down—everybody goes across—and in great white words of smoke in the sky tell everyone how I feel." On his love letters, Estlin often drew an elephant, which was still his favorite animal.

In the spring of 1933, Cummings was awarded a fellowship of fifteen hundred dollars from the Guggenheim Foundation, an organization that supports scholars and artists, to pay his expenses for a year while he composed a book of poems. The money was intended to fund work abroad, and since Marion had never been to Europe, he invited her to live with him in France. Estlin and Marion never married, but he introduced her to people as his wife, and by 1940 she had adopted the name Marion Morehouse Cummings.

The trip was fun from the start. Aboard ship was a troupe of African-American entertainers on their way to perform in Paris. One was a friend of Marion's, and the ocean crossing turned into a long party. In Paris, Estlin and Marion settled in a spacious apartment with a roof garden. He wrote, and she started modeling for *Paris Vogue* magazine.

They saw Ezra Pound and his wife, and another American, Lincoln Kirstein, who was a great champion of the arts. In 1927, while a student at Harvard, Kirstein founded a literary magazine, *Hound & Horn;* two years later he helped establish the Museum of Modern Art in New York City. Kirstein dreamed of starting an American ballet company, one with American dancers performing ballets created by Americans. He invited Cummings to write a ballet scenario based on American material. In return, he paid Cummings a hundred dollars a week and published some of his poems in *Hound & Horn*. Marion suggested the

Arts patron Lincoln Kirstein (*left*) discusses ideas for staging a ballet based on Shakespeare's *A Midsummer Night's Dream* with choreographer George Balanchine.

subject for the ballet: *Uncle Tom's Cabin,* the famous antislavery novel by Harriet Beecher Stowe.

Estlin loved introducing Marion to Paris, and she presented him to the friends she had there. Among them was Baron George Hoyningen-Huene, one of the great fashion photographers of the 1930s. The baron had been born in St. Petersburg, but like much of the Russian aristocracy, he had fled to save his life at the time of the Russian Revolution. He considered Marion "the most beautiful woman and the most poised in Paris," and Estlin dubbed him "a nice fellow." The baron owned an opulent villa in Tunisia, and he invited the Cummingses to vacation there.

Estlin felt his mind and muscles relax on the sun-baked North African coast, in a setting that offered both mountains and the seaside for sketching. From September through November, he and Marion slept through the hottest part of the day, from noon until three, and swam at a beach "uninhabited save for occasionally goats." They dined outdoors, as free-roaming camels munched on cactuses. "Everyone does exactly as everyone likes,including the sun and a full moon!" Cummings reported to his mother.

In December, when Estlin returned with Marion to New York, he had a finished book of poems and the start of his ballet scenario, *Tom,* in his suitcase. He eagerly submitted the poetry to publishers, but one after another told him no thanks. It made no difference that he was an established writer or that this collection contained some fine poems. During the Depression, hardly anyone was buying books, especially books of poetry. In the first half of 1934, Covici-Friede sold not a single copy of *Eimi* or the untitled book.

Some publishers rejected the book for another, more ominous, reason. Socialism was sacred to many writers and editors in the 1930s, and they wanted nothing to do with the man who had written *Eimi.* There were even a few writers who crossed the street if they saw Cummings approaching, to avoid speaking to him.

After fourteen publishers turned down the new book, Cummings decided to print it himself, using money from his mother to hire Sam Jacobs's Golden Eagle Press. He called this book *No Thanks,* and in it he printed the names of the fourteen publishers in a list shaped like a funeral urn.

No Thanks included poems that were lovely, playful, outrageous, and always fresh and new. In the first poem, Cummings took pleasure in the musical *O* sounds that John Keats had taught him to love:

mOOn Over tOwns mOOn
whisper
less creature huge grO
pingness

whO perfectly whO
flOat
newly alOne is
dreamest . . .

The large *O*s mimic the roundness of a ripe, full moon.

Cummings liked to joke that his poetry was "all done with mirrors," and this certainly seems true for the poem that begins, "r-p-o-p-h-e-s-s-a-g-r." Throughout the poem these letters hop about—"PPEGORHRASS," "gRrEaPsPhOs"—until they arrange themselves to reveal the jumping insect they describe: "grasshopper."

In a poem about dawn, Cummings describes the world changing from a place where objects barely have form in the weak, early light to one that is solid and awake:

as if as

if a mys
teriouSly("i am alive"

)
 brave

ly and(th
e moon's al-down)most whis
per(here)ingc r O

wing;ly:cry.be,gi N s agAains

t b
ecomin
gsky?t r e e s
!

One poem was so shocking for 1935 that instead of printing it, Sam Jacobs left a blank page, and Cummings wrote the poem by hand in just nine copies of *No Thanks*. This rhyming poem, which is printed in collections of Cummings's work today, begins, "the boys i mean are not refined / they go with girls who buck and bite. . . ." The speaker in this poem (who may or may not be the poet) uses a number of obscenities in his portrait of these boys and their girls, yet it appears that he admires their honest approach to life:

> they speak whatever's on their mind
> they do whatever's in their pants
> the boys i mean are not refined
> they shake the mountains when they dance

The literary world paid little attention to *No Thanks,* and Cummings sold very few copies. Earning a living as a writer or artist is often a struggle, but the Depression made it especially hard. Some creative people went to work for the Works Progress Administration (later called the Work Projects Administration), or WPA, a government agency formed in 1935 to give jobs to adults and reduce unemployment.

The WPA hired people to do all kinds of things: to clean up slums, lay out parks and playgrounds, and build airports, libraries, and schools. WPA artists painted murals in post offices and other public places, and WPA musicians played in community orchestras. Writers on the WPA payroll penned guidebooks to the forty-eight states and Washington, D.C., and interviewed former slaves and others for oral history projects. The WPA was one of a large group of agencies formed during the presidency of Franklin Delano Roosevelt that were intended to get the economy moving. Together these agencies and the laws that established them were known as the New Deal.

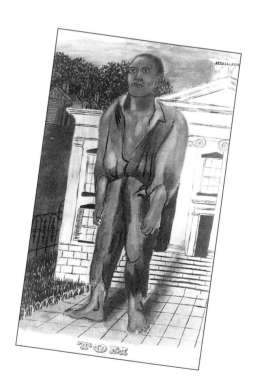

The artist Ben Shahn created this illustration for the frontispiece of *Tom*.

Young men in the Civilian Conservation Corps, a New Deal jobs program, combat a forest fire. Cummings thought that government-sponsored employment like this resembled Soviet collectivism.

New Deal programs did more than put people to work. They also protected the prices farmers received for their crops and livestock, brought electricity to rural areas, and insured bank deposits. One important New Deal program, Social Security, funded pensions for older men and women and financial aid to dependent mothers and children and the disabled.

Cummings had never cared much about national politics and rarely voted, but now his friends often heard him speak out against the New Deal. The "nude eel" looked too much like the public work programs he had seen in the USSR, he said. The government was assuming too much control of the economy. He called Roosevelt a communist sympathizer and warned that the United States was sliding into socialism. The friends shook their heads and told one another that Estlin's thinking was falling behind the times.

Yet his poetry was current and appealed to young people. One day in the spring of 1935, a letter came to Patchin Place from Helen Stewart and Dorothy Case, two students at Bennington College, then a small women's college in Vermont. The women invited Cummings to give a poetry reading at the school and offered him twenty-five dollars plus expenses. It was a small sum, but during the Depression every dollar helped, so Cummings agreed to go.

Helen Stewart planned to introduce their guest to the audience, but as the auditorium filled, she felt too nervous to speak to the crowd. It didn't matter, because Cummings needed no introduction. With the audience reciting his poem, "Buffalo Bill's / defunct," he simply walked onstage.

Helen and "Casey" became regular visitors to Joy Farm. They moved to Greenwich Village after graduating in 1936, and Helen's parents commissioned Cummings to paint her portrait. Like other young people who joined Cummings's circle of friends, they admired his dedication to art and to being himself. Paul Bowles, a composer who was twenty-five when he met Cummings in 1936, said that what he admired, "apart from his intelligence and talent, was his capacity for enjoying the act of living."

Not every writer was poor during the Depression. Some were earning large salaries writing film scripts in Hollywood. Among these was Eric Knight, author of the classic children's novel *Lassie Come-Home*, who had met Cummings in New York. Knight wrote to Cummings from California to urge him to come west and try his luck at screenwriting. Cummings listened, because somehow he had to make more money. He could not keep depending on his seventy-seven-year-old mother for support. He had earned less in 1934 than in any other year, and he had learned from Lincoln Kirstein that there would be no ballet *Tom*.

George Balanchine, the choreographer with Kirstein's new American Ballet Company, had rejected Cummings's scenario because it seemed like a work to be read rather than danced. Several composers, including Aaron Copland, had turned down Kirstein's offer to write the music for the ballet.

Was *Tom* more like a book than a ballet? Here is how Cummings described the enslaved people in a dance of religious ecstasy:

> the kneeling bodies begin together swaying, their asking arms meanwhile fall floatingly and rise; together the praying children women men prostrate slowly and slowly raise themselves; together they unkneel, together stand: yearningly around the always erect man [Tom] they whirl writhing upspiral and at his feet collapse together. . . .

And here are the "Human Bloodhounds," the dreaded slave catchers who earned a living capturing escaped African Americans:

everywhere seethes the almostdarkness with the stalkings with the findings with
the pouncings of luminously hither-and-thither spurting infrahuman figures. . . .

If *Tom* was meant to be read, then Cummings would arrange for it to be printed as
a book. He prevailed on an old acquaintance from Cambridge Latin School, who
now owned a publishing company, to print this small volume.

Meanwhile, Estlin and Marion were off to Hollywood. In the early summer of
1935, they found an apartment in Santa Monica, California, eleven blocks from the
Pacific Ocean. They loved Southern California's warm temperatures, flower-

Composer David Diamond wrote a complete ballet score for *Tom* and, in 1948, an orchestral piece inspired by *The Enormous Room*.

scented air, and shimmering beaches, and the Santa Monica Mountains inspired Estlin to paint. He soon figured out, though, that Hollywood was not the place for him. His cutting-edge poetry and prose had offered little preparation for script writing, and he hated the way profits drove the movie industry. It seemed that studios cared more about films that made money than scripts with literary worth. Movie people, a sour-tempered Cummings decided, were "distinguished numbskulls" and "morons." By late August, he and Marion had had enough of West Coast life, but they could not afford to leave until Rebecca Cummings wired them the money to come home.

They spent the fall at Joy Farm, and when New Hampshire turned cold, they went to 4 Patchin Place. Estlin lived in his studio, a large third-floor room, and Marion occupied a first-floor apartment. Estlin joined her for meals and relaxation and to receive guests, but he wrote, painted, and slept upstairs.

In early 1936, Marion and Estlin welcomed another young friend into the first-floor living room. David Diamond was a twenty-one-year-old composer at the start of his career. Diamond had been surprised to learn from Aaron Copland that no one had composed music for *Tom*, and he offered to write the score. He had seen, in Cummings's scenario, the story of *Uncle Tom's Cabin* told in movement. He concluded it was "a real ballet script," and he told Cummings, "You should have subtitled *Tom* 'a spectacle to be danced, sung and mimed.'" The only thing missing from *Tom*, Diamond said, was a spiritual for the slaves to sing, and he asked Cummings to write the lyrics to one. Cummings wrote the spiritual, and Diamond set to work on the score. When it was almost summer, the young composer went to Paris, hoping to persuade the French choreographer Leonide Massine to stage the ballet. Massine declined the offer, and although Diamond finished his score, *Tom* was never danced.

Cummings's career brought emotional ups and downs. Rejection of *Tom* by the ballet world disappointed him, but to be championed by a gifted young composer made his efforts worthwhile. Another dedicated fan was Charles "Cap" Pearce, a youthful editor at the publishing house Harcourt Brace. Pearce believed that Cummings was a major American poet but few people recognized his greatness because his books were hard to find. Pearce wanted to gather the best of Cummings's poetry in a single volume, so it could easily be appreciated.

Together Pearce and Cummings sifted through hundreds of poems. Cummings wanted the selection to represent "what I like,irrespective of whether it's obscene or unsetupable. What I don't like is,naturally,whatever I don't feel to be myself." He also told Pearce that "with few exceptions, my poems are essentially pictures." It was necessary to choose a "combination of typesize and papersize as will allow every picture to breathe its particular life . . . in its own private world." No lines were to be broken to be made to fit on the page, and each poem was to have a page to itself.

Pearce and Cummings selected poems from *Tulips and Chimneys, &, XLI Poems, is 5, ViVa*, and *No Thanks*. They also chose twenty-two new poems, including one that could have been Cummings's daily prayer:

> may my heart always be open to little
> birds who are the secrets of living
> whatever they sing is better than to know
> and if men should not hear them men are old. . . .

Cummings wrote an introduction to *Collected Poems* in which he spoke to the reader directly, as though he and the reader alone knew the secrets of living. "The poems to come are for you and for me and are not for mostpeople," he wrote. "What does being born mean to mostpeople? Catastrophe unmitigated. Socialrevolution. . . . Mostpeople fancy a guaranteed birthproof safetysuit of nondestructible selflessness. If mostpeople were born twice they'd probably call it dying."

Cummings and the reader were different. "We can never be born enough," he stated. "We are human beings;for whom birth is a supremely welcome mystery, the mystery of growing:the mystery which happens only and whenever we are faithful to ourselves."

"Miracles are to come," he promised. "With you I leave a remembrance of miracles:they are by somebody who can love and who shall be continually reborn."

(9)

T r u e   W a r s   A r e
N e v e r   W o n

ollected Poems did what Cap Pearce hoped it would do: it brought together a large number of Cummings's poems and established their author
as an important poet. "With all its failures and beauties, its clashing styles,
its brainsmashing complexities and moving simplicities, this is the poetry of a
man of complete artistic integrity," commented a critic in the *Saturday Review of
Literature.*

With the four-hundred-dollar advance payment from Harcourt Brace and
other earnings, Estlin and Marion spent two months in Europe, reaching London
in June 1937. Estlin occasionally heard from Elaine, and on this trip he and
Marion had tea with the MacDermots, who were living in England. They did not
see Nancy, then seventeen, who was at school in Vienna.

In London and Paris, everyone was talking about the possibility of war.
Through treaties signed in 1936 and 1937, Germany, Italy, and imperialist Japan
had formed an alliance known as the Axis Coalition. Under Chancellor Adolf
Hitler, Germany was building up its military might with the goal of ruling Europe
and other parts of the world. Hitler's Nazi party was founded on the belief that the
German, or "Aryan," people were superior to the rest of humanity.

The democratic nations of Europe did nothing when Nazi Germany occupied
Austria in March 1938. They viewed the move as an adjustment to the continental
balance of power that would appease Germany's lust for territory. A year later,
when Germany invaded Czechoslovakia, the policy of appeasement seemed less
plausible, however.

In the spring of 1939, Ezra Pound returned to the United States to receive an honorary degree from Hamilton College in Clinton, New York. When called upon to speak, Pound attacked the antifascist views of H. V. Kaltenborn, a journalist who was also present. Pound's behavior was becoming strange. He wrote articles supporting fascism for any magazine that would publish them, and rambling, confused letters to politicians, bankers, and professors. He picked arguments with his American friends about current events and monetary policy. "The man is sunk, in my opinion, unless he can shake the fog of Fascism out of his brain during the next few years," said William Carlos Williams.

When Pound came to 4 Patchin Place, Estlin and Marion found him changed. Not only did he talk nonstop, but he also made nasty remarks about Jews, who were subjected to violence and cruelty in German-controlled territory and targeted by the Nazis for extinction. He insisted that his ideas were correct and everyone else was mistaken. To Estlin he appeared "incredibly lonesome." Cummings abhorred the opinions Pound was expressing, but he remained a concerned and loyal friend. He kept his friends for life—just like his old clothes, he said.

On September 3, 1939, Great Britain and France declared war on Germany. Hitler continued his aggression nonetheless, taking control of Belgium and the Netherlands in May 1940. France fell to German forces in June, a turn of events that especially saddened Cummings. Britain valiantly fought on alone with weapons produced in the United States, and many Americans wondered whether the

Adolf Hitler salutes the crowd at a Nazi rally in Nuremberg, Germany, in 1934.

June 1940: German soldiers walk their bicycles around the Arc de Triomphe in Nazi-occupied Paris.

planes, warships, and guns coming out of their factories were signs that the United States was preparing to enter the war. At least publicly, Roosevelt followed a policy of neutrality, promising the nation, "Your boys are not going to be sent into any foreign wars."

For once, Cummings agreed with the president, but he didn't trust him. He suspected Roosevelt would change his mind. Cummings still saw no sense in war, which he called "the science of inefficiency." And when talk turned to patriotism and the obligation to fight for one's country, he announced, "The only nation to whom I owe allegiance is imagination." Cummings intended to sound clever, but he was speaking the truth. He usually paid no heed to world and national affairs and occupied his mind with creative questions.

His painting style had changed, and so had his poetry. He wrote less free verse now and more metered, rhyming poems. By 1940, he had enough new poetry for another book, *50 Poems*. One of the best-known poems in this collection celebrates the life of an individual, "anyone," who is ignored by his unthinking, conforming neighbors:

> anyone lived in a pretty how town
> (with up so floating many bells down)
> spring summer autumn winter
> he sang his didn't he danced his did.
>
> Women and men(both little and small)
> cared for anyone not at all
> they sowed their isn't they reaped their same
> sun moon stars rain

Cummings's anyone finds love with "noone," who shares his joy and grief, and together they grow old and die. The townspeople bury them side by side and return to their busy lives:

> Women and men(both dong and ding)
> summer autumn winter spring
> reaped their sowing and went their came
> sun moon stars rain

In one of the few free-verse poem-pictures in the book, words and letters turn and tumble like the autumn leaf they describe:

!blac
k
agains
t

(whi)
te sky
?t
rees whic
h fr

om droppe

d

,

le
af

a:;go

e
s wh
IrlI
N

·g

Although defense manufacturing was creating jobs and bringing the nation out of the Depression, the new book sat untouched on bookstore shelves, World events, not poetry, commanded people's attention. On December 7, 1941, Japan carried out a surprise attack on the U.S. naval base at Pearl Harbor, Hawaii, and nearly destroyed the American Pacific Fleet. The next day, President Roosevelt signed a declaration of war with Japan, and on December 11, Germany and Italy declared war on the United States. American forces would be sent to fight in Europe, where the Axis nations controlled much of the continent; in the Pacific, where Japan occupied Korea, Thailand, a large section of China, and other territory; and in North Africa, where the Italians and Germans acted as aggressors. The United States, Great Britain, and the nations that fought alongside them were known as the Allies.

As in France during World War I, Cummings witnessed hatred based on nationality. The U.S. government rounded up Japanese Americans on the West Coast—many of them U.S. citizens—and forced them to live in prison camps. His outrage found expression in his poetry, as in a poem that mimics intolerance based on ignorance:

> LISN bud LISN
>
> dem
>
> gud
>
> am
>
> lidl yelluh bas
>
> tuds weer goin
>
> duSIVILEYEzum

(If Cummings's meaning is unclear, try reading the lines aloud.)

In another poem of protest, he wrote:

> Bang is the meaning of a gun
> it is a man means No
> and(seeing something yes)will grin
> with pain You so&so
>
> true wars are never won

The antiwar poems appeared in yet another book, *1 X 1* [One Times One], which was published in 1944. For this book Cummings received the Shelley Memorial Award of six hundred seventy dollars from the Poetry Society of

America. Presenting the award to Cummings was Harold Vinal, president of the society, whose name Cummings had made free with in "Poem, or Beauty Hurts Mr. Vinal."

If some of Cummings's poems sounded cranky, it may be because he was in pain. He suffered from backaches that were often severe. In January 1942, a bone specialist in Boston diagnosed the problem as arthritis of the spine and fitted him with a custom-made corset. Cummings hated this uncomfortable device—"I feel like somebody living in a drain-pipe," he complained—but the corset reduced his pain, so he wore it.

Out of kindness, Estlin's old friend Sibley Watson paid the doctor's bill for the financially strapped Cummings; he also offered to pay the costs when Marion was hospitalized in early 1944 with mysterious pains in her arms, legs, and back. For twelve years, Estlin and Marion had never been apart. Now she spent weeks in a hospital bed, acutely ill, and doctors said she might never walk again. Estlin went to see her every day. He brought her flowers, wrote her letters, and drew her cartoons.

Marion was found to have rheumatoid arthritis, a far more serious condition than the one afflicting Estlin. By June, she was well enough to start exercising her inflamed joints in a pool, but she was too ill for the rustic life of Joy Farm, so Estlin spent three weeks there alone. The farm was a cheerless place without its "Guardian Angel." "The hilltop and all its inhabitants—its birds and crickets and butterflies and flowers—are lonely," he wrote to Marion.

Slowly, Marion improved. By December, she could get out of bed and walk on crutches, and by the end of January 1945, she was ready to continue treatment at home. And when summer came again, she went to Joy Farm with Estlin. Marion had taken up photography, and she worked to improve her picture-taking skills in the glorious mountain scenery.

One of Estlin's valentines to Marion. Cummings still drew elephants, his favorite animals, as he had in childhood.

Estlin and Marion were in New Hampshire when World War II ended. The German armed forces had surrendered to the Allies on May 8, 1945. The war in the Pacific ended three months later, after President Harry S. Truman ordered atomic bombs to be dropped on the Japanese cities of Hiroshima on August 6 and Nagasaki on August 9. Estimates of the number of people killed in these massive, unearthly explosions vary from 117,000 to 240,000. (The exact number is impossible to determine because many deaths from exposure to radiation occurred months or years later.) Japan announced its unconditional surrender on August 14, and although Cummings welcomed the return of peace, the atomic bombs convinced him that scientific knowledge had advanced more rapidly than awareness of its power, making the world a very dangerous place. Society was dominated by a "colossal lust for knowing," he said, "which threatens not simply to erase all past and present and future human existence but to annihilate (in the name of liberty) Life Herself."

Ezra Pound had spent the war years in Italy, making radio speeches denouncing Roosevelt, praising Hitler, and criticizing Jews. He was arrested in April 1945, as the Allies fought their way into Italy, and confined at the American Disciplinary Training Center at Pisa, a camp built to hold dangerous prisoners and deserters. In November, the U.S. government flew him to Washington, D.C., to face charges of treason; conviction could mean the death penalty. Pound, clearly in poor mental health, awaited trial in a hospital.

Many people wondered how a mind capable of creating exquisite poetry could harbor such ugly thoughts, and some asked whether it was right to read Pound's poetry at all. Cummings wrestled with these questions and tried to separate the poet he had befriended from the incoherent zealot Pound had become. He wrote in his journal, "To confuse these 2 persons(to try to makc 1 or whole out of them)is murderous nonsense." Publicly, Cummings defended Pound's freedom of thought and speech in the magazine *PM*. "Every artist's strictly illimitable country is himself," he wrote. "An artist who plays that country false"—who betrays his beliefs— "has committed suicide."

Pound's attorney came to Cummings's home to request further help. His client's medical bills were growing, but the government had seized Pound's money at the time of his arrest. Dorothy Pound, the poet's wife, had funds in England, but she didn't have access to them because wartime bans on the international transfer of money were still in place. Cummings, who had just received a thousand dollars for a painting from Sibley Watson, gave the money to Pound's attorney, explaining that he didn't need it. In truth, Cummings's generosity was much greater than it appeared. Marion also had high medical bills, Cummings's earnings were low, and it was rare that he sold a painting.

That winter, court-appointed psychiatrists determined that Pound was mentally unfit for trial. He was confined to a ward for the criminally insane at St. Elizabeth's Hospital in Washington.

Some of Cummings's other friends also had sad fates. Scofield Thayer had suffered a mental breakdown in 1926 and would remain hospitalized or under a doctor's care until his death in 1982. Hart Crane jumped overboard and drowned in waters off Cuba while sailing home from Mexico in March 1932. And Eric Knight joined the army and was killed in a plane crash in January 1943 while on his way to North Africa. Another death that affected Cummings was that of someone he had never met. George Herriman, the creator of *Krazy Kat,* died in April 1944. Cummings saved Herriman's obituary for the rest of his life.

Loss is part of living, but so is unexpected gladness. In the summer of 1946, Estlin learned from Billy James, an old Cambridge acquaintance who also vacationed in New Hampshire, that Nancy was staying at a place down the road from Joy Farm. Nancy was now twenty-five and married to Willard Roosevelt, a grandson of President Theodore Roosevelt, and had a year-old son. Estlin and Marion invited the Jameses and the Roosevelts to tea.

Nancy, who also wrote poetry, was excited to meet the poet whose books she admired and who had been married briefly to her mother. She thought she was meeting him for the first time, yet his voice sounded oddly familiar. It "seemed extraordinary, like a bell, like something from afar, almost echoing," she said. Nancy, who still thought Scofield Thayer was her father, was left to wonder.

A child lost and found is central to Cummings's short play *Santa Claus,* which was published just before Christmas 1946. Cummings's Santa Claus is a glum fellow who has "so much to give; and nobody will take." As the play opens, he is talking to that sinister character Death, who, wearing a mask of a human skull, advises him to get something to sell. They are living in "a world of salesmanship," Death tells Santa Claus. The public wants "knowledge without understanding," and if a salesman is a scientist, too, then his job is simple.

Death and Santa Claus exchange masks. Santa Claus becomes "Science" and sells shares of stock in a wheelmine. There is no such thing as a wheelmine, but because Science is selling, the public wants to buy. Desire for a wheelmine quickly takes hold, and one is built regardless of the consequences. Soon afterward, when miners are injured in an accident, an enraged mob turns on Science. Desperate to save himself from lynching, he turns to a little girl and asks, "Who am I?" The little girl, whose innocence allows her to see through masks, answers, "Santa Claus." "There ain't no Santa Claus!" the mob cries, and Santa Claus is saved because he doesn't exist.

Then Death and Santa Claus trade clothes. Santa Claus meets a despondent woman who welcomes him, believing him to be Death. She is about to surrender but holds back when his voice makes her think of her lost love. As soon as the woman chooses to live, the child dances onstage and into the woman's arms. Santa Claus removes his mask to reveal the face of a young man. Holding the child and kneeling to him, the woman says, "Ours." The play ends with a family reunited— a pretty wish.

Cummings was fifty-two when he wrote *Santa Claus*. He was still slender and had retained his youthful grin, but health problems made both him and Marion appear older than their years. Estlin's sister, Elizabeth, in contrast, remained healthy and vigorous. She had married Carlton Qualey, a history professor, and had two children. In September 1946, the Qualeys moved to Minnesota, where Carlton had found a teaching job, and Rebecca Cummings went to live with them. The poet's mother, born in 1859, was as stout and merry as ever. She'd endured several small strokes and a series of falls and broken bones, but she refused to dwell on illness or dying. She liked to say, "I may go anytime, or I may live to be a hundred!"

In January 1947, at the age of eighty-seven, she suffered a severe stroke that left her disabled. She spent a week in a Minnesota nursing home and then slipped into a coma and died. She was buried in Cambridge, alongside her husband. It comforted Estlin to hear his poetic tribute to his mother, "if there are any heavens . . . ," recited at her funeral. She was "an extraordinary human being, someone gifted with indomitable courage," he noted in a letter to Hildegarde Watson, Sibley Watson's wife.

If Rebecca Cummings died with one regret, it was this: she never got to know her oldest grandchild. Yet it looked as though Estlin might have a second chance for a relationship with his daughter. In 1947, Nancy wrote to Estlin and Marion to announce the birth of a baby girl. Nancy and her family now lived in Long

Rebecca Cummings
in old age, in the
living room at
Joy Farm.

Island City, New York, close to Manhattan, and Estlin offered to paint her portrait.

Nancy came for a sitting whenever she could arrange child-care. Marion was always present while Estlin painted, supposedly to answer the telephone and make his life peaceful in other ways. There was still no radio at 4 Patchin Place. "I have no and never had any and never shall have until having's obligatory(which God forbid!)radio," Cummings proclaimed. He forbade a vacuum cleaner, because he

A Cummings
self-portrait,
painted in 1947
and photographed by
Marion Morehouse
Cummings.

hated the noise, and asked Marion not to clean with bleach, because its odor upset his concentration. But Marion was also present during Nancy's visits to keep the conversation impersonal. She had discouraged Estlin from renewing contact with his child, and she was determined to limit Nancy's intrusion on their lives.

Estlin completed a small portrait in the spring of 1948, and that fall he undertook a larger painting of Nancy. During one of the final sittings, Marion got up to answer the door, and Nancy asked Estlin a question about Scofield Thayer. Estlin responded with a startling question of his own: "Did anyone ever tell you I was your father?" At first, Nancy thought Estlin was joking, but when Marion returned, he announced, "We know who we are."

As an adult, Nancy had tried to form a bond with Scofield Thayer, but his illness had prevented any closeness. Now she attempted to be a daughter to Cummings; however, he stifled her efforts. If she called him Father, he reminded her that his name was Estlin. It seemed that too much time had passed for Cummings to be a parent to this young woman. He could not be Santa Claus. He wrote in his journal, "while part of me is her tragic & immediate father, I am wholly and permanently someone else." Marion's jealousy also kept Nancy at a distance. Marion insisted that Nancy make appointments to come over and not simply drop in as family members often do. If Nancy telephoned, Marion answered and told her that Estlin was unavailable.

In August 1951, Nancy spent a week at Joy Farm without her family, sleeping at night in the studio where Cummings worked by day. One evening, Cummings forgot to put away his work, and Nancy studied the many versions of an unfinished poem that lay spread across his desk.

It was a mistake. When she commented to Cummings on his method of writing poetry, he let her know that she had violated his privacy. The next day, Marion told Nancy to leave. "You know how hard it is for your father to have anyone around while he is trying to work," Marion said. "It is time to go."

(1 0)

Such Mysteries

"The very thing which I'd have given my heart for 25 years ago, today knocks me down," Cummings said. It pained him not to be the father Nancy wanted him to be. He told her he was "very happy, that you can love me so richly"; yet at the same time he was "very miserable, that I must love you so poorly in return. For (as I've already tried to tell you) I'm a wholly selfish individual, whose work—or play—is his life." Estlin and Nancy stayed in touch, but they never formed a close bond.

Estlin was happiest now at Joy Farm. He delighted in colts born in spring, flocks of birds rising into the sunset, and the sliver of a new moon that promised renewal. Now he wrote about "the leaping greenly spirits of trees / and a blue true dream of sky," and how "spring follows winter: / as clover knows." Poems like these went into his book *Xaipe*, published in 1950. *Xaipe* is a Greek word meaning "rejoice," and is pronounced "KAI(as in Kaiser)rea(as in ready)," according to the author.

A book by Cummings would not be complete without daring feats of language, and *Xaipe* contained its share. Here is his poem about a cat taking a spill and recovering its poise, a scene familiar to anyone who has watched cats:

(im)c-a-t(mo)
b,I;l:e

FallleA

```
                        ps!fl
                        OattumblI

                        sh?dr
                        IftwhirlF
                        (Ul)(lY)
                        &&&

                        away wanders:exact
                        ly;as if
                        not
                        hing had,ever happ
                        ene

                             D
```

The eighth line even looks like a pair of cat's eyes.

This poem is not difficult to figure out, yet it proved too strange for William Carlos Williams, who questioned whether it was poetry at all. "I would reject it," Williams said. "I can't understand it. He's a serious man. So I struggle very hard with it—and I get no meaning at all."

Two other poems in *Xaipe* stirred up enormous controversy, not because of punctuation or words split and spliced together, but because of the particular words Cummings used. One of these poems begins:

> a kike is the most dangerous
> machine as yet invented . . .

And the other starts this way:

> one day a nigger
> caught in his hand
> a little star no bigger
> than not to understand . . .

(113)

Cummings at work on the porch at Joy Farm.

Friends begged Cummings to reconsider publishing these poems, and the book's editor pleaded with him to withdraw them, but he insisted that they stay. All the fuss perplexed him. The poems were commenting on prejudice, he pointed out, and not condoning it. He intended to show how derogatory words cause people to see others in terms of stereotypes rather than as individuals. "America(which turns Hungarian into 'hunky' & Irishman into 'mick' and Norwegian into 'squarehead')is to blame for 'kike,'" he said.

Many readers found the slurs hurtful nonetheless. The word *kike* especially caused pain in 1950, because the world was still grieving the murder of six million Jews in Nazi death camps. When it was announced in late 1950 that Cummings was to receive an award of five thousand dollars from the Academy of American Poets, a number of writers and critics felt compelled to speak out. Some labeled Cummings an anti-Semite. "Cummings as a writer is socially as vicious as he is poetically base," said Stanton Coblentz of the League for Sanity in Poetry, a group that endorsed traditional verse, who clearly was not a fan. William Carlos Williams defended Cummings as an artist even if he avoided comment on the offensive terms. "We give the artist freedom requiring only that he use it to say *Whatever He Chooses to Say*," Williams declared. "We do not suppress him when he happens to say something which we dislike or to which we are for various reasons officially or individually opposed."

Despite the debate over *Xaipe*, Cummings's reputation as a poet was growing. At fifty-six, he was at last enjoying financial security. In 1950, he accepted another distinguished prize, the Harriet Monroe Poetry Award from the University of Chicago, which came with five hundred dollars, and in February 1951, his aunt Jane died, leaving him seventeen thousand dollars from her estate. At the time of her death, Jane Cummings was ninety-seven and still lived at 104 Irving Street. Now the family home in Cambridge would be sold.

In 1951, Cummings also received a second Guggenheim Fellowship. Thirteen years had passed since he and Marion had last seen Europe, so they were excited to set sail in May for three months in Paris, Italy, and Greece. It was heartening to see bombed-out European cities rebuilding and to be welcomed everywhere as Americans, but travel was no longer the high adventure it had been in the past. Paris had become a different city from the one Cummings had known before the war. "The people haven't recovered their spirits," he observed. Parisians stood in long lines to buy rationed goods, and the Communist Party was active. It was easier to enjoy Italy now, without Mussolini, but the Cummingses found Greece to be hot, dry, and dusty. Their joints ached from hiking the hilly streets, and they both caught an intestinal virus.

Throughout the trip, Estlin's heart was at Joy Farm, "the one dearest thing to me in this world," and although Marion would have liked to stay in Europe, he arranged for them to sail home a month early. More and more, Cummings sheltered himself from the world and its people. "Now he lives in a second Enormous Room, this one of the imagination," observed William Carlos Williams.

The privacy of Joy Farm brought peace, but public life had its responsibilities. In 1952, Cummings received a letter from Professor John Finley of Harvard, inviting him to accept the Charles Eliot Norton Professorship for the 1952–53 school year. The professorship was one of the highest honors Harvard could bestow and came with a salary of fifteen thousand dollars. Cummings needed only to live in Cambridge from October through Christmas and from February through May, and to give six lectures. He accepted the post, and he and Marion rented a house near Harvard, but he fretted about the lectures. What in the world would he say? "Lecturing is presumably a form of teaching; and presumably a teacher is somebody who knows," he said. "I never did, and still don't, know. What has always fascinated me is not teaching, but learning."

Professor Finley said Harvard welcomed "freshness and individuality." Cummings could give traditional lectures on a topic like the nature of poetry, or he could discuss specific poems in detail. If he preferred, he could simply talk about himself or combine his lectures with poetry reading. After much worry, Cummings decided to give six "nonlectures" in which he addressed the question, "who, as a writer, am I?"

The Sanders Theatre, the same hall where Cummings had talked about "The New Art" in 1915, was packed on October 25, 1952, the night of the first nonlecture. Some students mounted the fire escape, hoping to crawl through a window. Old friends came, including Betty Thaxter Hubbard, Estlin's early playmate, and Tex Wilson, who was a painter living in Roxbury, Massachusetts. Those lucky enough to get a view saw Cummings walk onstage with exaggerated posture, owing to the corset he wore, and sit stiffly behind a desk. The crowd fell silent, and every ear strained to hear the famous inventive poet.

Cummings may have looked starchy, but his speech was warm and captivating. In the broad New England accent that he never lost, he took his listeners back to the Cambridge of his childhood and introduced them to his father and mother. He led them through his years of self-discovery at Harvard and in New York and Paris, and he talked about the poet's responsibility. "It's you—and nobody else—who determine your destiny and decide your fate. Nobody else can be alive for you," he told the assembled students and friends. "If you can take it, take it—and be."

He read from his own writings, from *The Enormous Room, Eimi, Him,* and *Santa Claus,* and he concluded each talk by reciting a few of his favorite poems. Some were his own, and some were verses he held dearer than his own, by Shakespeare, Keats, Dante, and other great poets. "He was irreverent, funny, handsome, brilliant," said a Radcliffe student who attended the nonlectures. "His appearance at Harvard was absolutely thrilling to many of us who had read his books. To catch even a glimpse of the great man was extraordinary."

It turned out that Cummings loved performing. He had been a natural entertainer all his life, amazing friends and relatives with his steady flow of words. Poetry readings became a way to connect with students as well as add to his income. Throughout the 1950s, he appeared on college campuses, in museum auditoriums, and in settings like the YM-YWHA Poetry Center in New York City. He typically sat at a table, behind a microphone, with a desk lamp casting light on his books. He read for a half hour from his plays and prose works and then presented a selection of poems. Through his readings, Cummings became one of the best-known poets in the United States.

Even people who rarely read poetry knew some of his lines. In the early 1950s, the movie star Marilyn Monroe picked up a book by Cummings while browsing in a bookstore. "There was apprehension in her eyes when she began to read, the look of a student afraid to be caught out, but suddenly she laughed in a thoroughly unaffected way at the small surprising turn in the poem about the lame balloon man—'and it's spring!'" recalled Monroe's husband at the time, playwright Arthur Miller. "'And it's spring!' she kept repeating on our way out to the car, laughing again as though she had been handed an unexpected gift."

In 1954, the year he turned sixty, all of Cummings's published poetry appeared in a single book, *Poems, 1923–1954.* The following year, the National Book Award for Poetry, a prize that honors great American writing, went to Wallace Stevens for his *Collected Poems,* but Cummings received a special citation for his book. This meant he was a close runner-up. The citation angered Cummings, who thought that he should have won. In his opinion, Stevens, an insurance-company executive, was a businessman and not an artist.

But there were other ways to be recognized and rewarded. Cummings was invited to be the official poet of the 1957 Boston Arts Festival, an annual celebration of music, drama, painting, and literature, held over several weeks in June. He would perform just once, and the planning committee asked that he write a new poem for the festival. His poem could be on any subject, and of any length.

On any subject at all? Cummings seldom read newspapers, but in the fall of 1956, he was following events in Hungary, a communist nation dominated by the Soviet Union since the end of World War II. The Hungarian constitution, adopted in 1949, resembled that of the Soviet Union. The government had confiscated the property of private citizens and churches, and students were forced to study Russian and the philosophies of Karl Marx and Vladimir Lenin. A large and powerful secret police force had the authority to arrest citizens for any reason and send them to brutal prison camps.

On October 23, 1956, a group of students and writers, unhappy with the regime and their country's weak economy, posted a list of demands. They called for open elections, a new economic system free from Soviet control, and freedom of speech, expression, and the press. They staged a demonstration in the Hungarian capital, Budapest, that began peacefully. Then the police fired on unarmed students, and the protesters fought back with rocks, sticks, and anything else they could throw. The government called out soldiers to restore order, but many of them joined the rebellion instead.

Soviet troops entered the city on October 24, and things quieted down. A new government was established, with a new prime minister, Imre Nagy. Then, in defiance of the USSR, Nagy freed political prisoners, abolished the secret police, promised free elections, and declared Hungary a neutral nation.

The USSR was not about to lose its grip on Hungary. Before dawn on November 4, while most Hungarians slept, Soviet tanks rolled into Budapest and launched a surprise attack. The Hungarian military fought back, and Nagy appealed to the United Nations and the free world for help. "Our ship is sinking. The light vanishes. The shadows grow darker from hour to hour," said a radio broadcaster. "People of the world, save us. S-O-S. Help, help, help."

No help came. Thousands of people died in the defeated revolt, and Nagy went into hiding. (He would be executed by the Soviets in 1958.)

Cummings had always hated war, but now it distressed him that the United States, "(alias earth's richest nation)—the sworn enemy of brute force, the foremost friend of democratic freedom, perpetually dedicated to an unconditional defense of all oppressed peoples," had watched freedom die in a small country and done nothing. The failure to respond troubled him most at Thanksgiving, when Americans feasted on their nation's bounty and gave thanks for their own liberty.

"I was so frantic and sick, I felt I would die if I couldn't do something in this situation," he said. His outrage drove him to his typewriter, and he poured his feelings into a poem:

> a monstering horror swallows
> this unworld me by you
> as the god of our fathers' fathers bows
> to a which that walks like a who . . .
>
> so rah-rah-rah democracy
> let's all be thankful as hell
> and bury the statue of liberty
> (because it begins to smell)

When Cummings submitted "Thanksgiving (1956)" to the planners of the Boston Arts Festival, they faced a dilemma. Rejecting the poem was against their policy, yet its theme of political protest was opposed to the festival's holiday spirit. They asked Cummings gently if he would mind submitting something else.

This time, he cooperated. He substituted "i am a little church(no great cathedral)," a religious poem in which he seems to describe himself approaching the end of life:

> —i do not worry if briefer days grow briefest,
> i am not sorry when sun and rain make april . . .
>
> i am a little church(far from the frantic
> world with its rapture and anguish)at peace with nature
> —i do not worry if longer nights grow longest . . .

Hungarians look at an enormous statue of Soviet leader
Joseph Stalin after demonstrators in Budapest pulled it
to the ground on October 24, 1956.

Seven thousand people sat on folding chairs or stretched out on the lawn of
Boston's Public Garden to hear Cummings read his poetry on the hot night of
June 23, 1957. "The big crowd loved him. He read slowly, meaningfully, lov-
ingly—lingering on each syllable without losing for an instant the drive and surge
of his poems," wrote a reviewer in *Harper's* magazine. "And his slow, clear gift of
full value to every word unfolded to the ear the rhyme and rhythm that his verses
may not convey to the eye."

The listeners warmly applauded each poem. Then, toward the end of the program, Cummings read, "a monstering horror swallows / the living spirit . . . ," and
the audience gasped. It was true that he had withdrawn "Thanksgiving (1956)" as

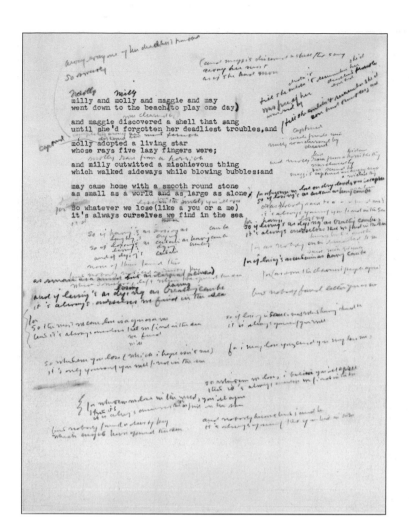

A worksheet for the poem "maggie and milly and molly and may." Cummings filled more than twenty sheets of paper with typed and penciled revisions before achieving the finished version, which he included in *95 Poems*:

maggie and milly and molly and may
went down to the beach(to play one day)

and maggie discovered a shell that sang
so sweetly she couldn't remember her
troubles,and

milly befriended a stranded star
whose rays five languid fingers were;

and molly was chased by a horrible thing
which raced sideways while blowing
bubbles:and

may came home with a smooth round stone
as small as the world and as large as alone.

For whatever we lose(like a you or a me)
it's always ourselves we find in the sea.

Ezra Pound (*right*) at the time of his release from St. Elizabeth's Hospital, with friend and fellow poet William Carlos Williams.

the official festival poem, but he had remained true to his ideals for sixty-two years, and he would not start censoring himself now. He finished the poem, and the crowd erupted in clapping and cheering. Cummings made "Thanksgiving (1956)" part of his poetry readings from then on, and audiences always responded with instant applause.

Invitations continued to come. The University of California at Los Angeles invited Cummings to give the Ewing Lectures, a series presented each year by a distinguished American or British writer, on November 18 and 20, 1957. He consented to go because he would receive twenty-five hundred dollars, but writing these lectures caused him even more stress than the nonlectures did. Once again, he reached into the past. He tried to write about his time with the ambulance corps, the conscientious objector he called Olaf, Scofield Thayer and the *Dial,* and his friendship with Ezra Pound, but he got nowhere. His stomach ached, a rash spread over his hands, and he had trouble sleeping at night. He canceled the appearance at UCLA and all his fall readings.

A doctor who had examined Cummings in 1955 described him as a "thin, high-strung, middle-aged man who does not appear to be ill," but now medical tests revealed a large polyp in his colon. It was a benign growth that could turn cancerous, so it needed to be removed. Cummings underwent surgery at Strong Memorial Hospital in Rochester, New York, on October 10, and recuperated at the nearby home of Sibley and Hildegarde Watson. The surgeon offered him medicine to ease his pain, but Cummings refused it. He wanted to feel everything life offered, including physical suffering, he said. Ten days passed before he was well enough to step outside and walk to the corner, and not until six months later was all the tenderness gone.

Life looked a little brighter in 1958. Yale University gave Cummings the Bollingen Prize in Poetry, an award that in previous years had gone to Ezra Pound,

William Carlos Williams, and Wallace Stevens. In 1958, Cummings published *95 Poems,* the last book of poetry to appear in his lifetime.

Some of the ninety-five were poems whose beauty arose from their simplicity:

l(a

le
af
fa

ll

s)
one
l

iness

Others commented on nature—on the mountains and skies of New Hampshire or on snow falling in Washington Square. Cummings once told Ezra Pound that he had learned a great deal from observing "a very few birds(who have honoured me with their friendship)," so here were poems about hummingbirds, blue jays, and English sparrows.

Many of the poems reflect the thoughts of a mature adult meditating on love, the passing of time, and the brevity of life:

—how fortunate are you and i,whose home
is timelessness:we who have wandered down
from fragrant mountains of eternal now

to frolic in such mysteries as birth
and death a day(or maybe even less)

The year 1958 was also when the U.S. attorney general dropped all charges against Ezra Pound, and the court dismissed his indictment for treason. Released from the hospital, Pound returned to Italy a broken man.

Cummings, too, saw Europe again. In May 1959, he and Marion went to Ireland, where Marion came down with a cold and spent most of the time in bed. In the spring of 1960, they went to Greece to see Nancy, who was living there and who had been ill. Nancy had divorced Willard Roosevelt and in 1954 had married Kevin Andrews, the author of two books based on his research and travels in Greece. Nancy now had four children.

Estlin's back ached constantly throughout the trip, and Marion, still jealous, treated Nancy and Kevin rudely. Estlin was alone with Nancy only briefly, when they walked together along a street. He smiled at her and said, "You love your children very much," but he could think of little else to say. He never knew how much the visit saddened Nancy, who had yearned all her life for a father's love.

Estlin's world was growing smaller. In New York each morning, he walked in

Estlin and Marion at Joy Farm, summer 1962.
This is the last photograph ever taken of the couple.

(124)

Washington Square to observe people and nature. He came home and climbed the stairs to his studio, where he painted, wrote poems, or worked on the captions for a book of photographs that Marion was assembling. Patchin Place was changing; a fourteen-story apartment building was going up right outside the window of Estlin's studio.

Joy Farm was changing as well. Estlin permitted a heating system to be installed so he and Marion could stay there later in the year. He also let electricians put in wiring for a refrigerator and a darkroom for Marion. At Joy Farm, too, Estlin kept to a daily routine. Every morning he filled a hummingbird feeder with sweetened water and took a stroll to watch for animals and inspect flowers. On September 2, 1962, he noted in his journal that Marion's delphiniums had lost their blossoms and gone to seed, "But yesterday I noticed a lovely light-blue (& far smaller) blossomer who'd come to her beauty all alone!"

He spent that afternoon out beside the barn, splitting wood. The job done, he sharpened the ax on a grindstone, making it ready for next time, as his father had taught him so many years ago. He walked to the farmhouse and went upstairs, and then Marion heard him fall. She found him lying in a hallway, unconscious. An ambulance rushed him to a hospital, where doctors determined that he had suffered a massive stroke. Cummings died at one-fifteen a.m. on September 3, at the age of sixty-seven. That day, all the flags in the nearby town of Madison, New Hampshire, flew at half staff.

The funeral was small and private. Nancy's two teenage children, Simon and Elizabeth Roosevelt, were the only relatives to attend. Edward Estlin Cummings was buried in Boston's Forest Hills Cemetery, near his parents. Marion Morehouse Cummings, heartbroken over her loss, died of cancer in 1969; Nancy Thayer Andrews spent most of her long life in London.

No American poet has ever been more playful than E. E. Cummings, and none has been more skillful at arranging words on a page. Many poets have imitated his style, but their attempts only prove what a masterful stylist Cummings was. His final book of poetry, *73 Poems,* was published after his death, in 1963. In 1965, four of the fairy tales he wrote for Nancy as a little girl were published as a children's book.

In one of these stories, a fairy lives on the farthest star, and the people of the stars and air bring their troubles to him. One morning, millions of angry people come to complain about an old man on the moon who keeps saying "why." "The millions of troubled angry people cried out together in a chorus, 'We want you to help us all quickly and if you don't we'll all go mad!'"

The fairy flies to the moon, where he finds a "little very very very very very very very old man" sitting on a church steeple. He says to the man, "Listen to me:if you say why again,you'll fall from the moon all the way to the earth."

And the little very old man smiled;and looking at the faerie,he said "why?" and he fell millions and millions and millions of deep cool new beautiful miles(and with every part of a mile he became a little younger;first he became a not very old man and next a middle-aged man and then a young man and a boy and finally a child)until,just as he gently touched the earth,he was about to be born.

Estlin and Elizabeth Cummings in New Hampshire with Rex.

All books and articles cited here are listed in the bibliography.

Epigraph

E. E. Cummings, "(Who: / Loves . . .)" is from Cummings, 1958, p. 432.

Chapter 1. little i

p. 2   E. E. Cummings, "I was welcomed as no son . . ." is from Cummings, 1972, p. 11.

p. 2   E. E. Cummings, "a crack shot & a famous fly-fisherman . . ." is from Cummings, 1972, p. 8.

p. 2   Edward Cummings, "Anything worth doing at all . . ." and "smile before breakfast . . ." are quoted in Kennedy, p. 100.

p. 2   E. E. Cummings, "the most amazing person I've ever met" and "Never have I encountered anyone more joyous . . ." are from Cummings, 1972, p. 11.

p. 3   Elizabeth Cummings, "Mother knew how to enjoy people . . ." is quoted in Kennedy, p. 17.

p. 4   James Russell Lowell, "And what is so rare . . ." is from Lowell, James Russell, p. 3.

p. 5   "to stimulate the higher and nobler instincts . . ." is from Lowell, James Russell, p. vii.

p. 5   E. E. Cummings, "Oh my little birdie oh . . ." is quoted in Kennedy, p. 36.

p. 5   E. E. Cummings, "I did not decide to become a poet . . ." is quoted in Norman, p. 24.

p. 5   Lucretia Cummings, "I never rest easy . . ." is quoted in Norman, p. 22.

p. 5   Elizabeth Cummings, "My brother was great fun . . ." is quoted in Norman, pp. 20–21.

p. 6   Clarke, "Jane, let's have some ruddy gore!" is quoted in Cummings, 1972, p. 27.

p. 6   Hubbard, "I spent most of my time . . ." is quoted in Culhane, p. 169.

p. 7   Elizabeth Cummings, "My father liked to have us play . . ." is quoted in Norman, p. 18.

p. 8   "ten years without the curse of an open saloon" is from *The No-License Years in Cambridge,* p. v.

p. 8   "disorder was on the increase . . ." is from Gilman, p. 91.

p. 8   Beach, "Catholics have come to love Protestants . . ." is from Gilman, pp. 95–96.

p. 9   Baldwin, "is a most loveable little boy . . ." is quoted in Kennedy, p. 29.

p. 9   Emerson, "By the rude bridge that arched the flood . . ." is from Emerson, p. 2.

p. 10   "God forgive us for our short Cummings" is quoted in Kennedy, p. 6.

p. 10   E. E. Cummings, "The dying embers of the fire glow . . ." is quoted in Kennedy, p. 43.

p. 10   "must never write a line . . ." and "must use such rhymes . . ." are from Hood, p. 15.

p. 11   Hood, "The poet gives to the world . . ." is from Hood, p. 11.

p. 11   Herriman, "T'was a long time ago . . ." is from Herriman, p. 25.

p. 12   E. E. Cummings, ". . . you have given your silent best . . ." is quoted in Kennedy, p. 50.

p. 12   Edward Cummings, "I keep them to remind me . . ." is quoted in Kennedy, p. 49.

Chapter 2. An Unknowable Bird

p. 14   Eliot, "Harvard University undertakes . . ." is from Langstaff, p. 9.

p. 16   Keats, "I saw thee sitting . . ." is from Abrams, p. 1861.

p. 18   "disused golf clubs and bags," "a dynamited suit of Japanese armor," and "orderly heap of broken violins," are quoted in Adams, p. 429.

p. 18   Amy Lowell, "Why do the lilies goggle . . ." is from Lowell, Amy, p. 216.

p. 18   E. E. Cummings, "mysterious" is quoted in Kennedy, p. 81.

p. 19   E. E. Cummings, "He lived for the honor of art" is quoted in Kennedy, p. 80.

p. 19   E. E. Cummings, "Officially, Harvard presented me . . ." is from Cummings, 1972, p. 47.

p. 20   E. E. Cummings, "with the love which is worship" and "with the love that gives battle" are quoted in Kennedy, p. 103.

p. 20   Edward Cummings, "Anything worth doing at all . . ." is quoted in Kennedy, p. 100.

p. 21   Keats, "I am certain of nothing . . ." is from Scott, p. 54.

p. 21   E. E. Cummings, "an unknown and unknowable bird . . ." is from Cummings, 1972, p. 51.

p. 21   Dos Passos, "No one could help . . ." and "He had an old-fashioned . . ." are from Dos Passos, "P. S. to Dean Briggs," pp. 48–49.

p. 21   E. E. Cummings, "a courageous and genuine exploration . . ." is from Firmage, 1958, p. 22.

p. 22   "Is that our president's sister's poetry . . ." and Damon, "Meanwhile, the president's face . . ." are from Damon, p. 312.

p. 22   Amy Lowell, "Little cramped words . . ." is from Lowell, Amy, pp. 209–10.

p. 22   E. E. Cummings, "superb of its kind. . . ." is from Firmage, 1958, p. 20.

p. 22   E. E. Cummings, "sound painting" is from Firmage, 1958, p. 21.

p. 22   Stein, "Elephants beaten with candy . . ." is from Stein, pp. 15–16.

p. 22   E. E. Cummings, "How much of all this . . ." is from Firmage, 1958, p. 22.

Chapter 3. High and Clear Adventure

p. 23   "Literature especially in Greek and English" is quoted in Kennedy, p. 53.

p. 25   Scofield Thayer, "really corking" is quoted in Kennedy, p. 191.

p. 25   Eliot, "Five-foot Shelf of Books" is from "Bunk, in Faded Gingham," p. 84.

p. 25   E. E. Cummings, "warming a wooden chair . . ." is quoted in Kennedy, p. 129.

p. 26   Tate, "We were young . . ." is quoted in Unterecker, p. 358.

p. 26   "You hear eager discussion of everything . . ." and "You will suddenly hear a young man . . ." are from Shackleton, pp. 355–56.

p. 27   E. E. Cummings, "I can't express to you . . ." is quoted in Kennedy, p. 131.

p. 28   E. E. Cummings, "In New York I also breathed . . ." is from Cummings, 1972, p. 52.

p. 28   Dos Passos, "Cummings would deliver himself . . ." is quoted in Wetzsteon, p. 458.

p. 29   "every available weapon" is quoted in Cashman, p. 480.

p. 31   Brown, "the most entertaining man . . ." is quoted in Kennedy, p. 3.

p. 31   E. E. Cummings, "divine section of eternity" is quoted in Kennedy, p. 140.

p. 32   E. E. Cummings, "Now, finally and first . . ." is from Cummings, 1972, p. 53.

p. 32   E. E. Cummings, "average" is quoted in Sawyer-Lauçanno, p. 113.

p. 32   "sticktuitiveness and enthusiasm" is quoted in Dupee and Stade, p. 29.

p. 32   Anderson, "how they do things in America" and "to keep away from those dirty Frenchmen" are quoted in Cummings, 1934, p. 3.

p. 33   E. E. Cummings, "unlovely" is from Cummings, 1934, p. 3.

p. 33   E. E. Cummings, "a high and clear adventure" is from Cummings, 1934, p. 7.

p. 33   Brown, "I think we're going to prison . . ." is quoted in Cummings, 1934, p. 12.

p. 33   minister of health, "You are aware that your friend . . ." is quoted in Cummings, 1934, p. 16.

p. 34   E. E. Cummings, "I am not" is from Cummings, 1934, p. 16.

p. 34   minister of health, "We have the very best reason . . ." is quoted in Cummings, 1934, p. 18.

p. 34   E. E. Cummings, *"J'aime beaucoup les francais"* is from Cummings, 1934, p. 19.

p. 34   minister of health, "It is impossible to love Frenchmen . . ." is quoted in Cummings, 1934, p. 19.

p. 34   minister of health, "I am sorry for you . . ." is quoted in Cummings, 1934, p. 20.

p. 35   E. E. Cummings, "I am having *the time of my life!*" is from Dupee and Stade, p. 38.

Chapter 4. Love and Telegrams; Poems and Soldiering

p. 36   Norton, "EDWARD E. CUMMINGS HAS BEEN PUT IN A CONCENTRATION CAMP . . ." is quoted in Norman, p. 76.

p. 36   Edward Cummings, "No child of your mother . . ." is quoted in Kennedy, p. 153.

p. 36   Rebecca Cummings, "TAKE THE GREATEST CARE FOR MY SAKE" is quoted in Kennedy, p. 153.

p. 37   Edward Cummings, "crime against American citizenship . . ." is quoted in Norman, p. 94.

p. 37   Edward Cummings, "I do not speak for my son alone . . ." is quoted in Norman, p. 95.

p. 37   Edward Cummings, "sacred in the eyes of Frenchmen" is quoted in Norman, p. 96.

p. 38   E. E. Cummings, "impossibly tall, incomparably tall," "the noises of America," and "nearingly throbbed with smokes . . ." are from Cummings, 1934, pp. 331–32.

p. 41   E. E. Cummings, "Another's and Belongs to Another Person" is quoted in Kennedy, p. 193.

p. 41   E. E. Cummings, "The artist is merely . . ." is from Dupee and Stade, p. 52.

p. 42   E. E. Cummings, "Mine is the perspiration . . ." is from Dupee and Stade, p. 51.

p. 42   E. E. Cummings, "a semi-liquid demiviscous pudding-of-rubber-heels" is from Dupee and Stade, p. 50.

p. 42   Drill instructor, "Stick it in the bellies . . ." is quoted in Dupee and Stade, p. 53.

p. 43   Base commander, "What would you do . . ." and pacifist soldier, "Sir, I have no sister" are quoted in Kennedy, p. 320.

p. 44   E. E. Cummings, "a lot of circles . . ." and "more swimmingish" are quoted in Kennedy, p. 204.

p. 44   "The brilliant sally in color . . ." is quoted in Sawyer-Lauçanno, p. 152.

p. 44   E. E. Cummings and Brown, "fishhooks and pajamas," "lilacs and monkeywrenches," and "squirrels and efficiency" are quoted in Kidder, p. 17.

p. 45   E. E. Cummings, "withdrew from reality" is quoted in Sawyer-Lauçanno, p. 163.

p. 46   E. E. Cummings, "Elaine Thayer's daughter looks just like a doll . . ." is quoted in Sawyer-Lauçanno, p. 163.

p. 47   E. E. Cummings, "OF Some One" and "OF something" are from "Gaston Lachaise," in Firmage, 1958, p. 19.

p. 47   E. E. Cummings, "a phenomenon" is from Firmage, 1958, p. 23.

p. 47   E. E. Cummings, "In his enormous and exquisite way . . ." is from Firmage, 1958, p. 20.

p. 47   E. E. Cummings, "Lachaise's work is the absolutely authentic expression . . ." is from Firmage, 1958, p. 16.

Chapter 5. Firstness

p. 49   E. E. Cummings, "what amounts to my own printing-press . . ." and "my Firstness" are from Dupee and Stade, p. 71.

p. 49   "paintings by E. E. Cummings . . ." is quoted in Kennedy, p. 211.

p. 50   E. E. Cummings, "every paragraph a thing . . ." and "In every inch there is a binding rhythm . . ." are quoted in Kennedy, p. 212.

p. 51   Edward Cummings, "I am sure now . . ." is quoted in Kennedy, p. 213.

p. 51   E. E. Cummings, "a year or a century" is quoted in Kennedy, p. 215.

p. 51   E. E. Cummings, "a boy barefooting . . ." is from a notebook in the E. E. Cummings Collection at the Houghton Library, Harvard University (bMS Am 1832.7 [31]).

p. 51   E. E. Cummings, "I wish you could have seen the feria" is from Dupee and Stade, p. 76.

p. 52   E. E. Cummings, "Never be AFRAID" is from Dupee and Stade, p. 85.

p. 52   E. E. Cummings, *There is no such thing . . .*" is from Dupee and Stade, p. 84.

p. 52   E. E. Cummings, "To Hell with everything . . ." is from Dupee and Stade, p. 86.

p. 53   Pound, "In a Station of the Metro" is from Pound, p. 50.

p. 53   E. E. Cummings, "Mr. Ezra Pound is a man . . ." is quoted in Ahearn, pp. 1–2.

p. 53   Pound, "clever" is quoted in Wilhelm, p. 42.

p. 55   E. E. Cummings, "E. E. Cummings (not E. Estlin . . .)" is quoted in Sawyer-Lauçanno, p. 195.

p. 55   E. E. Cummings, "life's most magical moment" is quoted in Kennedy, p. 240.

p. 56   "Mr. Cummings has written a terrible book . . ." is quoted in Norman, p. 110.

p. 56   "I feel as if I had been rooting . . ." is quoted in Norman, p. 109.

p. 57   E. E. Cummings, "Take me up into your mind . . ." is from Cummings, 1934, p. 293.

p. 58   E. E. Cummings, "Things which are always inside of us . . ." is from Cummings, 1934, p. 231.

p. 60   "He responds so eagerly and unconstrainedly . . ." is from Wilson, "Wallace Stevens and E. E. Cummings," Modern American Poetry.

p. 60   "The poet always seems to be having . . ." is from Monroe, "Flare and Blare," Modern American Poetry.

p. 60   "His poems are hideous on the page" is from Wilson, Modern American Poetry.

p. 60   "eccentric system of typography" is from Monroe, Modern American Poetry.

p. 60   Brown, "because he has carried over . . ." and "the poems of E. E. Cummings . . ." are from Brown, "On *Tulips & Chimneys*," Modern American Poetry.

Chapter 6. Griefs of Joy

p. 62   E. E. Cummings, "i am nearest happiness" and "i do no work . . ." are quoted is Sawyer-Lauçanno, p. 239.

p. 63   Elaine Cummings, "I know where I stand . . ." and "like a child" are quoted in Sawyer-Lauçanno, p. 244.

p. 63   E. E. Cummings, "give her the divorce . . ." is quoted in Kennedy, p. 259.

p. 63   E. E. Cummings, "I consider myself beaten . . ." is quoted in Kidder, p. 45.

p. 64   E. E. Cummings, "Goodbye dear . . ." is quoted in Sawyer-Lauçanno, p. 266.

p. 65   E. E. Cummings, "In losing the church . . . ," "only a small part of you . . . ," and "Now(for the first time . . ." are quoted in Sawyer-Lauçanno, p. 284.

p. 65   Edward Cummings, "If you feel that way . . ." is quoted in Sawyer-Lauçanno, p. 284.

p. 65   E. E. Cummings, "harmless" is quoted in Kidder, p. 36.

p. 67   E. E. Cummings, "Crane's mind was no bigger . . ." is quoted in Brunner, "Hart Crane: Biographical Sketch," Modern American Poetry.

p. 67   Crane, "a permanently beautiful thing" is from Hammer and Weber, p. 99.

p. 67   Crane, "only cared to take . . ." is from Hammer and Weber, p. 329.

p. 68   Crane, "If I had my way . . ." is from Hammer and Weber, p. 352.

p. 68   MacDermot, "Even if Elaine . . ." is quoted in Kennedy, p. 274.

p. 68   E. E. Cummings, "would not have one chance . . ." is quoted in Sawyer-Lauçanno, p. 273.

p. 68   E. E. Cummings, "the inner fringes . . ." is quoted in Kennedy, p. 277.

p. 68   E. E. Cummings, "obsessed by Making," "If a poet is anybody . . . ," "Whereas nonmakers must content themselves . . . ," and "rejoices in a purely irresistible . . ." are from Firmage, 1994, p. 221.

p. 69   E. E. Cummings, "the most alive aspect . . ." is from Firmage, 1965, p. 154.

p. 71   E. E. Cummings, "an entirely beautiful body . . ." is from Firmage, 1965, pp. 161–62.

p. 71   E. E. Cummings, "singularly uncheerful" is from Firmage, 1965, p. 165.

p. 71   Dos Passos, "to fuse the two halves . . ." is from Dos Passos, 1926, pp. 159–60.

p. 73   Rebecca Cummings, "You see?" is quoted in Sawyer-Lauçanno, p. 305.

Chapter 7. The High Wire

p. 74   Weird sisters, "We call our hippopotamus . . . ," "I wish my husband . . . ," and "Of course it's a bother . . ." are from Cummings, 1927, p. 1.

p. 74   Him, "Imagine a human being . . ." is from Cummings, 1927, p. 10.

p. 74   Him, "I am this trick . . ." is from Cummings, 1927, p. 11.

p. 75   Light, "was around all the time . . . ," "When the actors wanted . . . ," and "His greatest characteristic . . ." are quoted in Norman, p. 217.

p. 75   E. E. Cummings, "*him* isn't a comedy . . ." and "DON'T TRY TO UNDERSTAND . . ." are quoted in Norman, pp. 222–23.

p. 76   "fatiguing, pretentious and empty" and "incoherent, illiterate, preposterous . . ." are quoted in Sawyer-Lauçanno, p. 320.

p. 76   "projected himself across . . ." is quoted in Norman, pp. 223–24.

p. 76   "Now, if Mr. Cummings . . ." is quoted in Kennedy, p. 296.

p. 76   Light, "I am very proud . . ." and "We gave the bird . . ." are quoted in Sawyer-Lauçanno, p. 321.

p. 77   Williams, "I shall not forget . . ." and "birds in the nest . . ." are from Williams, p. 259.

p. 77   E. E. Cummings, "looking forward into the past . . ." is from Cummings, 1927, frontispiece.

p. 78   Rebecca Cummings, "I have been . . ." and E. E. Cummings, "She looked pale . . ." are quoted in Sawyer-Lauçanno, p. 309.

p. 80   E. E. Cummings, "2 clowns,sad,costumeless . . ." is quoted in Kennedy, p. 313.

p. 80   E. E. Cummings, "a world of Was . . ." is from Cummings, 1958, p. 8.

p. 81   E. E. Cummings, "Russia, I felt . . . ," "they hate by merely . . . ," and "hate by categorying . . ." are from Cummings, 1934, p. viii.

p. 86   Anne Cummings, "my puny husband" and "I want that property," are quoted in Kennedy, p. 325.

p. 86   E. E. Cummings, "Yes, she can have . . ." and "Everybody is to lie low . . ." are quoted in Sawyer-Lauçanno, pp. 351-52.

Chapter 8. Never Born Enough

p. 87   E. E. Cummings, "'A' as in a . . ." is from Cummings, 1934, p. vii.

p. 87   E. E. Cummings, "nonmen" and "unbanklike bank" are from Cummings, 1958, p. 21.

p. 87   E. E. Cummings, "facefacefaceface . . ." is from Cummings, 1958, pp. 240–241.

p. 89   "The Worst Book of the Month" is quoted in Norman, p. 273.

p. 90   Moore, "a large poem" is quoted in Norman, p. 265.

p. 90   Pound, "Oh well Whell hell . . ." and "The longer a work is . . ." are quoted in Norman, pp. 275–76.

p. 90   Morehouse, "You're such a wonderfully . . ." is quoted in Kennedy, p. 340.

p. 92   Hoyningen-Huene, "the most beautiful woman . . ." is quoted in Dupee and Stade, p. 123.

p. 92   E. E. Cummings, "a nice fellow" is from Dupee and Stade, p. 123.

p. 92   E. E. Cummings, "uninhabited save for . . ." and "Everyone does exactly . . ." are from Dupee and Stade, pp. 124–25.

p. 93   E. E. Cummings, "all done with mirrors" is quoted in Kidder, p. 107.

p. 95   E. E. Cummings, "nude eel" is quoted in Kennedy, p. 376.

p. 96   Bowles, "apart from his intelligence . . ." is quoted in Sawyer-Lauçanno, p. 410.

p. 96   E. E. Cummings, "the kneeling bodies . . ." is from Cummings, 1935, p. 11.

p. 97   E. E. Cummings, "everywhere seethes the almostdarkness . . ." is from Cummings, 1935, p. 14.

p. 98   E. E. Cummings, "distinguished numbskulls" and "morons," are quoted in Kennedy, p. 367.

p. 98   Diamond, "a real ballet script" and "You should have subtitled . . ." are quoted in Kennedy, p. 372.

p. 99   E. E. Cummings, "what I like . . . ," "my poems are essentially pictures," and "combination of typesize . . ." are quoted in Sawyer-Lauçanno, p. 411.

p. 99 E. E. Cummings, "The poems to come . . . ," "What does being born . . . ," "We can never be born enough," "We are human beings . . . ," and "Miracles are to come . . ." are from Firmage, 1994, p. 461.

Chapter 9. True Wars Are Never Won

p. 100 "With all its failures and beauties . . ." is quoted in Kennedy, p. 382.

p. 101 Williams, "The man is sunk . . ." is quoted in Ackroyd, p. 79.

p. 101 E. E. Cummings, "incredibly lonesome" is quoted in Kennedy, p. 387.

p. 102 Franklin D. Roosevelt, "Your boys are not going . . ." is quoted in "Teaching with Documents: Documents Related to Churchill and FDR," U.S. National Archives and Records Administration.

p. 102 E. E. Cummings, "The science of inefficiency . . ." and "The only nation to whom I owe . . ." are quoted in Sawyer-Lauçanno, p. 441.

p. 105 E. E. Cummings, "I feel like somebody . . ." is quoted in Sawyer-Lauçanno, pp. 441–42.

p. 105 E. E. Cummings, "Guardian Angel" and "The hilltop and all . . ." are quoted in Sawyer-Lauçanno, p. 451.

p. 106 E. E. Cummings, "colossal lust for knowing . . ." is from Cummings, 1972, p. 103.

p. 106 E. E. Cummings, "To confuse these 2 persons . . ." is quoted in Sawyer-Lauçanno, p. 465.

p. 106 E. E. Cummings, "Every artist's strictly illimitable country . . ." is from Firmage, 1965, p. 313.

p. 107 Nancy Thayer Roosevelt, "seemed extraordinary, like a bell . . ." is quoted in Kennedy, p. 417.

p. 107 E. E. Cummings, "so much to give . . ." and "a world of salesmanship" are quoted in Cummings, 1972, p. 104.

p. 108 E. E. Cummings, "Who am I?," "Santa Claus," and "There ain't no Santa Claus," are quoted in Cummings, 1972, p. 108.

p. 108 E. E. Cummings, "Ours" is quoted in Cummings, 1972, p. 110.

p. 108 Rebecca Cummings, "I may go anytime . . ." is quoted in Kennedy, p. 412.

p. 108 E. E. Cummings, "an extraordinary human being . . ." is quoted in Sawyer-Lauçanno, p. 472.

p. 109 E. E. Cummings, "I have no and never had . . ." is quoted in Sawyer-Lauçanno, p. 431.

p. 110 E. E. Cummings, "Did anyone ever tell you . . ." is quoted in Sawyer-Lauçanno, p. 470.

p. 110 E. E. Cummings, "We know who we are" is quoted in Kennedy, p. 420.

p. 111 E. E. Cummings, "while part of me is her tragic . . ." is quoted in Sawyer-Lauçanno, p. 472.

p. 111 Marion Cummings, "You know how hard it is . . ." is quoted in Kennedy, p. 429.

Chapter 10. Such Mysteries

p. 112   E. E. Cummings, "The very thing which I'd have given . . ." is quoted in Kennedy, p. 426.

p. 112   E. E. Cummings, "very happy, that you can love me . . ." and "very miserable, that I must love you . . ." is quoted in Kennedy, p. 427.

p. 112   E. E. Cummings, "KAI(as in Kaiser) . . ." is quoted in Kidder, p. 175.

p. 113   Williams, "I would reject it . . ." is quoted in Kidder, p. 191.

p. 115   E. E. Cummings, "America(which turns Hungarian into 'hunky' . . ." is quoted in Sawyer-Lauçanno, p. 482.

p. 115   Coblentz, "Cummings as a writer . . ." is quoted in Norman, p. 319.

p. 115   Williams, "We give the artist freedom . . ." is quoted in Sawyer-Lauçanno, p. 483.

p. 115   E. E. Cummings, "The people haven't recovered . . ." is quoted in Sawyer-Lauçanno, p. 492.

p. 116   E. E. Cummings, "the one dearest thing to me . . ." is quoted in Sawyer-Lauçanno, p. 493.

p. 116   Williams, "Now he lives in a second . . ." is quoted in Sawyer-Lauçanno, p. 504.

p. 116   E. E. Cummings, "Lecturing is presumably a form . . ." is from Cummings, 1972, p. 3.

p. 116   Finley, "freshness and individuality . . ." is quoted in Norman, p. 343.

p. 116   E. E. Cummings, "who, as a writer, am I?" is from Cummings, 1972, p. 110.

p. 117   E. E. Cummings, "It's you—and nobody else . . ." is from Cummings, 1972, p. 24.

p. 117   "He was irreverent, funny . . ." is quoted in Sawyer-Lauçanno, p. 506.

p. 117   Miller, "There was apprehension . . ." is quoted in Sawyer-Lauçanno, pp. 507–508.

p. 118   "Our ship is sinking . . ." is quoted in Ake, p. 48.

p. 119   E. E. Cummings, "(alias earth's richest nation) . . ." is quoted in Kennedy, pp. 453–454.

p. 119   E. E. Cummings, "I was so frantic and sick . . ." is quoted in Kidder, p. 207.

p. 120   "The big crowd loved him . . ." and "And his slow, clear gift . . ." are quoted in Kennedy, p. 457.

p. 122   "thin, high-strung, middle-aged man . . ." is quoted in Kennedy, p. 460.

p. 123   E. E. Cummings, "a very few birds . . ." is quoted in Kidder, p. 212.

p. 124   E. E. Cummings, "You love your children very much . . ." is quoted in Kennedy, p. 474.

p. 125   E. E. Cummings, "But yesterday I noticed a lovely . . ." is quoted in Kennedy, p. 484.

p. 125   E. E. Cummings, "The millions of troubled angry . . ." is from Cummings, 1965, p. 8.

p. 126   E. E. Cummings, "little very very very very . . ." is from Cummings, 1965, p. 12.

p. 126   E. E. Cummings, "Listen to me . . ." and "And the little very old man . . ." are from Cummings, 1965, p. 14.

glossary

abstract art: Art that relies on pattern, color, and form for expression, rather than the realistic representation of objects, people, or scenes.

allegory: A story in which the characters and occurrences stand for people, events, or ideas on a different level. In this way, an allegory tells a story that has a deeper meaning, which is often religious, moral, or political. A religious or moral allegory usually teaches a lesson, but a political allegory may satirize public affairs.

alliteration: Close repetition of a consonant sound for effect in poetry or prose. (Repetition of a vowel sound is called *assonance.*)

cadence: The rhythm of written or spoken language caused by the sequence of accented and unaccented syllables.

couplet: Two lines of poetry that form a unit, either alone or as part of a longer poem. The verses in a couplet frequently rhyme and have the same meter. Also, they often express a complete thought (see poem 10 in *95 Poems:* "For whatever we lose(like a you or a me) / it's always ourselves we find in the sea").

cubism: An artistic movement that revolutionized European painting and sculpture in the early twentieth century. Instead of depicting people or objects from one angle, in the traditional way, cubists presented several views or surfaces simultaneously.

epithalamion: A poem written in celebration of a wedding. The word *epithalamion* is derived from the Greek *epithalamios,* meaning "at the bridal chamber."

free verse: Poetry in which meter and line length vary and in which there is no apparent rhyme scheme. Free verse gained popularity in the twentieth century.

imagery: The words or phrases in a work of literature that appeal to the five senses. Writers use imagery to create vivid descriptions and to evoke feelings or memories in the reader that are associated with a particular object or experience. Imagery often takes the form of *simile* or *metaphor*.

imagism: A movement in early-twentieth-century poetry. Imagists used succinct, clear language to create sharp mental pictures, and avoided generalities.

metaphor: An implied comparison of two dissimilar things expressed as though they are one and the same. A writer employing metaphor defines the qualities of one thing by equating it with another (see poem XLIII in *ViVa:* "eyes which are really petals").

meter: The sound pattern that gives poetry its rhythm. Meter depends on the number of syllables in a line and the fact that only some syllables are stressed, or accented, in speech. The most common meters have names based on the number and pattern of stresses in a line. In iambic pentameter, the meter most often used in English, there are ten syllables per line, with unaccented and accented syllables alternating. Cummings frequently wrote his sonnets in iambic pentameter (see poem XIV in *ViVa:* "what time is it i wonder never mind").

rhyme: Words whose endings sound identical or very much alike are said to rhyme. In poetry, rhyme refers to the similar placement of rhyming words in two or more lines. The pattern of rhyming words in a poem is called its *rhyme scheme*.

scenario: An outline of the plot of a play, opera, or ballet. A scenario describes in detail the settings, sequence of action, and characters. It may also include notes on scenery and special effects.

simile: A comparison of two dissimilar things, employing the word *like* or *as* (see "Puella Mea": "the world was like a song / heard behind a golden door").

sonnet: A fourteen-line poem that usually rhymes. There are several patterns of rhyme for sonnets. One of the most popular forms, the Shakespearean sonnet, contains three four-line stanzas and ends with a rhyming couplet that comments on what has come before. In a Petrarchan sonnet, named for the Italian poet Petrarch, the first eight lines pose a question or problem, and the final six lines resolve it.

stanza: Two or more lines forming a section of a poem. Stanzas are separated from one another by space. In many poems, they have the same number of lines and the same meter and rhyme scheme. Like a paragraph in prose, a stanza may introduce a new thought.

stream of consciousness: The attempt to capture, in writing, thoughts, emotions, and impressions in the order that they pass through a character's mind. Cummings employed the stream-of-consciousness technique in *Eimi*.

style: The unique way in which one writer or artist approaches his or her work. Writers make choices with regard to vocabulary, the arrangement of words, and line or sentence length when considering how to set forth ideas or achieve an effect. Together, these choices constitute style. Other kinds of artists face different stylistic choices; painters, for example, make decisions about color and composition. A person's style can be as distinct as his or her personality.

syntax: The way words and phrases are arranged to form sentences.

theme: A main point or governing idea. The universality of human experience is a theme in Cummings's poem "anyone lived in a pretty how town" (poem 29, *50 Poems*).

verse: The word *verse* can be a synonym for poetry, or it can mean a single line in a poem.

selected bibliography

Abrams, M. H., ed. *The Norton Anthology of English Literature,* 3rd ed. New York: W. W. Norton and Co., 1975.

Ackroyd, Peter. *Ezra Pound.* London: Thames and Hudson, 1980.

Adams, Laurie Schneider. *A History of Western Art.* Madison, Wisc.: Brown and Benchmark, 1994.

Ahearn, Barry, ed. *Pound/Cummings: The Correspondence of Ezra Pound and E. E. Cummings.* Ann Arbor: University of Michigan Press, 1996.

Ake, Anne. *Hungary.* San Diego: Lucent Books, 2003.

Brunner, Edward, comp. "Hart Crane: Biographical Sketch," Modern American Poetry, Cary Nelson, ed., http://www.english.uiuc.edu/maps/poets/a_f/crane/bio.htm (accessed August 11, 2005).

"Bunk, in Faded Gingham." *Harvard Magazine,* September–October 2001, p. 84.

Cashman, Sean Dennis. *America in the Age of the Titans: The Progressive Era and World War I.* New York: New York University Press, 1988.

Culhane, John. *The American Circus: An Illustrated History.* New York: Henry Holt and Co., 1990.

Cummings, E. E. *Eimi.* New York: Grove Press, 1958 (first published in 1933).

———. *The Enormous Room.* New York: The Modern Library, 1934 (first published in 1922).

———. *Fairy Tales.* New York: Harcourt, Brace and World, 1965.

———. *Him.* New York: Boni and Liveright, 1927.

———. *i: six nonlectures.* Cambridge: Harvard University Press, 1972 (first published in 1953).

———. *Tom.* New York: Arrow Editions, 1935.

Damon, S. Foster. *Amy Lowell: A Chronicle.* Boston: Houghton Mifflin, 1935.

Dos Passos, John. *The Garbage Man: A Parade with Shouting.* New York: Harper and Brothers, 1926.

———. "P.S. to Dean Briggs," in David Aloian, ed. *College in a Yard II.* Cambridge: Harvard Alumni Association, 1985.

Dupee, F. W., and George Stade, eds. *Selected Letters of E. E. Cummings.* New York: Harcourt, Brace and World, 1969.

Emerson, Ralph Waldo. *The Best of Ralph Waldo Emerson.* New York: Walter J. Black, 1941.

Firmage, George J., ed. *E. E. Cummings: Complete Poems, 1904–1962,* Centennial ed. New York: Liveright, 1994.

———. *E. E. Cummings: A Miscellany.* New York: Argophyle Press, 1958.

———. *E. E. Cummings: A Miscellany Revised.* New York: October House, 1965.

Gilman, Arthur, ed. *The Cambridge of Eighteen Hundred and Ninety-Six.* Cambridge: Riverside Press, 1896.

Hammer, Langdon, and Brom Weber, eds. *O My Land, My Friends: The Selected Letters of Hart Crane.* New York: Four Walls Eight Windows, 1997.

Herriman, George. *Krazy Kat.* New York: Madison Square Press, 1969.

Hood, Tom. *The Rhymester: or, The Rules of Rhyme.* New York: D. Appleton and Co., 1882.

Kennedy, Richard S. *Dreams in the Mirror: A Biography of E. E. Cummings.* New York: Liveright, 1980.

Kidder, Rushworth M. *E. E. Cummings: An Introduction to the Poetry.* New York: Columbia University Press, 1979.

Langstaff, John Brett, ed. *Harvard of Today from the Undergraduate Point of View.* Cambridge: Harvard Federation of Territorial Clubs at the Harvard Union, 1913.

Lowell, Amy. *Complete Poetical Works.* Boston: Houghton Mifflin, 1955.

Lowell, James Russell. *The Vision of Sir Launfal.* Boston: Palmer Co., 1910.

Modern American Poetry, Cary Nelson, ed., http://www.english.uiuc.edu/maps/poets/a_f/-cummings/reviews.htm (accessed August 11, 2005).

The No-License Years in Cambridge. Cambridge: University Press, 1898.

Norman, Charles. *E. E. Cummings: The Magic-Maker.* Boston: Little, Brown and Co., 1972.

Pound, Ezra. *Lustra of Ezra Pound, with Earlier Poems.* New York: Alfred A. Knopf, 1917.

Sawyer-Lauçanno, Christopher. *E. E. Cummings: A Biography.* Naperville, Ill.: Sourcebooks, 2004.

Scott, Grant F., ed. *Selected Letters of John Keats.* Cambridge, Mass.: Harvard University Press, 2002.

Shackleton, Robert. *The Book of New York.* Philadelphia: Penn Publishing Co., 1917.

Stein, Gertrude. *Tender Buttons.* Mineola, N.Y.: Dover Publications, 1997 (first published in 1914).

"Teaching with Documents: Documents Related to Churchill and FDR," U. S. National Archives and Records Administration, http://www.archives.gov/education/lessons/-fdrchurchill/index.html (accessed September 8, 2005).

Unterecker, John. *Voyager: A Life of Hart Crane.* New York: Farrar, Straus and Giroux, 1969.

Wetzsteon, Ross. *Republic of Dreams.* New York: Simon and Schuster, 2002.

Wilhelm, J. J. *Ezra Pound: The Tragic Years.* University Park, Penn.: Pennsylvania State University Press, 1994.

Williams, William Carlos. *Autobiography.* New York: Random House, 1951.

Wilson, Edmund. "Wallace Stevens and E. E. Cummings." *New Republic* 38 (1924): 102–103, Modern American Poetry, Cary Nelson, ed., http://www.english.uiuc.edu/maps/poets/a_f/-cummings/reviews.htm (accessed July 30, 2005).

major published works of E. E. Cummings

Poetry

Tulips and Chimneys. New York: T. Seltzer, 1923.

XLI Poems. New York: Dial Press, 1925.

&. Privately published, 1925.

is 5. New York: Boni and Liveright, 1926.

W (ViVa). New York: Horace Liveright, 1931.

No Thanks. New York: Golden Eagle Press, 1935.

Collected Poems. New York: Harcourt Brace and Co., 1938.

50 Poems. New York: Duell, Sloan and Pearce, 1940.

1 X 1. New York: Henry Holt, 1944.

Xaipe. New York: Oxford University Press, 1950.

Poems 1923–1954. New York: Harcourt Brace and Co., 1954.

95 Poems. New York: Harcourt Brace and Co., 1958.

73 Poems. New York: Harcourt, Brace and World, 1963.

Prose

The Enormous Room. New York: Boni and Liveright, 1922.

[no title]. New York: Covici-Friede, 1930.

Eimi. New York: Covici-Friede, 1933.

Fairy Tales. New York: Harcourt, Brace and World, 1965.

Works for the Stage

Him. New York: Boni and Liveright, 1927.

Tom. New York: Arrow Editions, 1935.

Santa Claus. New York: Henry Holt, 1946.

Pictorial Works

CIOPW. New York: Covici Friede, 1931.

Adventures in Value. New York: Harcourt, Brace and World, 1962 (photographs by Marion Morehouse).

photo credits

index

Note: Page numbers in **bold** type refer to illustrations.